HARDPRESS.NET
HOME OF HARD-TO-FIND BOOKS

Terisina. the Lovers' Quarrel. Faithful and Forsaken. Wild Water Pond. the Pic-Nic. Chatelar. Lady Betty's Pocketbook. Insurance and Assurance. the Album. Benedetti's Adieu. Authors and Editors. the Moorish Barque
by Robert Sulivan

Address:
HardPress
8345 NW 66TH ST #2561
MIAMI FL 33166-2626
USA
Email: info@hardpress.net

FLITTINGS OF FANCY.

BY

ROBERT SULIVAN, ESQ.

" Black spirits and white,
Red spirits and grey ;
Mingle, mingle, mingle,
You that mingle may."
MACBETH.

IN TWO VOLUMES.

VOL. I.

LONDON:

HENRY COLBURN, PUBLISHER,

13, GREAT MARLBOROUGH STREET.

1837.

LONDON:

F. SHOBERL, JUN., LEICESTER STREET, LEICESTER SQUARE.

ADVERTISEMENT.

The tales, &c., which compose these volumes have, with a few exceptions, been published singly, at various dates, and in various ways. They are now collected, partly in consequence of the favours bestowed upon such of them as chanced to fall into the hands of reviewers, and partly because certain compilers of miscellanies have, from time to time, paid some little piece the compliment of a reprint. The Author intrudes this word of explanation in the hope that it may plead his excuse for the incongruous character of Fancies which were the fitful occupation of an idle life, and certainly never intended to Flit in company.

CONTENTS

OF

THE FIRST VOLUME.

FLITTINGS OF FANCY.

TERESINA.

> As easy may'st thou fall
> A drop of water in the breaking gulph,
> And take unmingled thence that drop again,
> As take from me thyself.
> *Comedy of Errors.*

THE traveller who has spent his winter in Rome will not forget how much of his enjoyment in the contemplation of modern art was derived from the numerous students from the North, domiciliated under the general description of the German school. They have a devotion to their calling, which makes it interesting to all who come in contact with them ; and the pride which they take in each other's genius, and the liberality of their mutual assistance, are traits sufficiently unusual amongst rivals to be worthy of admiration. My mornings were generally passed with one or other of them, and I was deep in the mysteries of half the unfinished pictures and statues of Rome — with their destinations and every thing relating to them.

The great patron, I found, and the one for whom they were all the most proud to labour, was a nobleman of the country, the Marchese di ————. They spoke his name as a word of triumph, and praised him as though he had been one of the fraternity. Some few particulars which I accidentally heard of him awakened a curiosity to hear more, and by degrees I became possessed of his history.

Many years previous to the time of which I am speaking, there laboured, in a small studio on the Monte Cavallo, a young German student in sculpture. Like his fellows, he was seldom aware at the beginning of the month of the source from whence means were to be derived for carrying him to the end of it;—but in talent they allowed him to stand above them. Still his chief employment was to toil upon the works of artists of older standing, and to confer fame whilst he received the wages of mere labour. Thus the genius of Frederic was known only to his familiar associates, and the original exercise of it was, of necessity, confined to the hours which others devoted to repose or to festa days, when scarcely another hand was at work in the whole capital.

Yet, with all this resistance of every enjoyment but study, and notwithstanding the obscure prospect of fame beyond the circle in which he already possessed it, Frederic had too much of the energy of genius, and too intense a delight in the search for beauty, to feel depressed. True, his countenance had the pale hue and the knitted brows of reflection, but its handsome character was heightened by an animated feeling for all things of intellectual interest, and his heart was always free enough from selfish care to be acutely sensible to the concerns of others. Whenever the light but manly figure of Frederic made its rare appearance amongst his more jovial friends, it was the signal for increased hilarity and a double forgetfulness of their hardships. There were few of them whose works had not benefited by his taste, and few who, while he never was seen in more pretending costume than his workman's cap and blouse, had not felt his off-hand, un-calculating generosity.

With such a character, amongst those so capable of duly appreciating him, it was no wonder if he found a ready reception from the few acquaintance whom he chanced to make in society more general. These consisted, for the most part, merely of the indigent, but, in many cases, well-born families established in charge of the palaces of public show, to the absentee or straightened possessors of which they might bear some remote affinity. In one of these temples to the genius of ancient days, Frederic professed to have found matter more conducive to excellence in his art than in any other which was open to him ;—according to him, there were vestibules and galleries which contained the pride of Greece, and, according to his friends, there were more private apart-ments which contained the pride of Rome.

Both of these statements were correct. The palazzo belonged to the Marchese di ———, a nobleman of great wealth but retired habits, which caused him to spend his time chiefly amongst the peasantry of his estate, leaving the splendid abode in question to a branch of his family which had shared in the general decay of his country. To this branch belonged the blossom alluded to. In the course of his visits to the mutilated statues and basso-relievos, Frederic had discovered a living work of perfection, which was destined to be a subject of more devoted study than all the wonders that marble had yet produced.

Teresina had just arrived at an age to make her friends sensible of her peculiar situation. She was, unhappily, too highly-born to be disposed of in any of the various ways which were open to the daughters of the simple citizen, and the dependent state of her parents rendered it next to impossible that she would ever be raised beyond it. She had sprung up amidst ruin, and would there, in all probability, fade neglected away. At the same time, the young Roman possessed the ardent feelings of her country in a degree as far above the common order as were her pale and dark-eyed beauty and the proud style of her perfect symmetry.

The knowledge that she was an object of painful concern subdued her spirit to an early habit of sadness, and the absence of youthful pastime left her the leisure and inclination to store her mind in a manner which rendered it still more sensitive. Few were the more fortunate of Rome's maiden beauties who could compare with her in refined acquirements; but her superiority was not a matter of congratulation; it only heightened her unfitness for her lot.

Both Teresina and the young German were early in discovering that they had met in each other, for the first time, the capability of mutual comprehension and mutual feeling. The commencement of their acquaintance had been confined to an inclination of the head, as they occasionally encountered upon the richly-ornamented terraces of the palace garden, the one musing over classic balustrades of inlaid marble, storied pedestals, and statues of whatever was most enchanting in history or fable ; the other, retiring with the sweet wild witnesses of a Roman spring, which burst forth spontaneously from the neglected plot — the rim of the sculptured fountain, the ruined wall of ages more remote. The city, with its domes and columns of a thousand tales—the blood-stained battle-field, the huge and melancholy Campagna—the Tiber, with its unknown treasures—and the distant mountains, from Soracte to the sea, with their cities of unknown origin—all brought their deep associations to aid entrancing odours and the triumphs of genius in disposing the mind to a keener perception of beauty, and the heart to a more intense feeling for it. Teresina, in her simple, sober-coloured drapery, with her downcast stateliness and maiden occupation, seemed the chosen model for a Psyche—the very spirit that had inspired a Phidias.

Commencements like these generally lead to something more important. Accidents were not wanting to bring them to the exchange of an occasional word. Afterwards, Frederic began a small copy of the Naïad on the fountain, and Teresina was requested to draw near and bestow her timid approbation. In such a scene, with those deep blue sunny skies above, those golden meteors gliding through the bright waters at their feet, the rainbow shedding its many-coloured glory from the spray that danced above their heads—with no subject of converse but the grace of an exquisite chisel, the lines of beauty, the tender traits of sentiment; it was no great stretch of fancy in such a pair to dream themselves in realms beyond the reach of sorrow; no surprising lapse of memory, if they forgot for the time the cold calculations of a world to which both were so little indebted.

The timid and the modest are, perhaps, the most ready to receive perilous impressions; for it is rarely that such characters are not the result of warm affections. The meetings between Teresina and Frederic were no longer caused by accident. She knew the moment of his release from labour, and, whether by the blaze of the bright spring morning, or the shades of its dewy sunset, her form was amongst the statues, her feeling beneath the cypress. She asked not if this was love—no matter *what* it was. She never could be anything to Frederic. The thought of hanging a disastrous load on his arduous path to fame never once occurred to her. She never could be anything to any one else, for who could be worth the reservation of her heart, where her merit was to be measured by Fortune? It was enough to find that life had, at last, a source of interest, a solitary sensation of bliss. It harmed none, and could not injure herself; for what happiness did she risk!

The feelings of Frederic were not so devoid of plan, though that plan was mainly supported by chimeras. His only chance of possessing Teresina was by a rise in reputation, which should atone for his want of birth; and the enthusiasm of his passion and his profession already foresaw such miraculous events as had never before occurred, excepting in the brain of a German lover. Alas! love has been called a stimulant to exertion; but, perhaps, it is more frequently an impediment. The mind of Frederic was occupied by one object solely, and that was the attainment of his end, and not the means. His toil grew wearisome, his hour of bliss was anticipated, and his reputation, instead of advancing, was likely to decline. A few weeks made him sensible of the necessity for some desperate exertion, or for the resignation of the hopes which had now become part of his existence. Whilst it was in his power to forget at any moment the pains of life with a being whose purity seemed placed on earth by accident, and who did not attempt to conceal that she had no thought beyond him, the temptation was not to be resisted. His energies could only be rightly applied by depriving himself of it altogether. His art must be pursued elsewhere.

At the time he had come to this conclusion, a sculptor of eminence was about to change the scene of his labours during the summer months to the comparatively cool retreat of Carrara. Frederic's resolution was put to the test by an invitation to assist him. His views might be answered beyond his expectation. He might be removed to the very mine from which he was to work out his fame. He gave his answer with a struggle, and the same evening saw him once more a wanderer beneath a few bright planets, and amongst the snowy gleams and graceful shadows of all that art could reach of beauty and divinity.

" Frederic," said a voice, soft, clear, and celestial, as though it had proceeded from one of those fabled inhabitants of the sky ; " I did not expect you to-night, but am here because I would be where you have been."

" Alas ! Teresina, and such, for I know not how long a time, is all the intercourse that will subsist between us. It is the will of Fortune that we part. I see the star-light trembling in your eyes, when I would look to you for courage. We never yet have spoken of the feeling by which our hearts are united, for in your guileless countenance I have fancied that I read the secret more clearly than your tongue could tell it. These bonds are love—wild, enthusiastic, unchangeable, as our natures. It has made our happiness ; it depends upon ourselves whether it is to make our misery. I depart in search of fame and fortune. It may not be vanity, if I declare to you (for what I breathe in *your* ear is no more than thinking aloud) that I feel within me the qualities to secure them. Then, when we meet again, we shall bless the pains of this parting hour as having led to joys which now we dare not dream of."

Teresina's experience in the world was merely infantine, and to rise from obscurity

and poverty to rank and wealth was a circumstance so out of the nature of things, especially
in Italy, where conditions only altered to decay, that she listened to the project of Frederic
in despair.

" Part !" she exclaimed with a low tremor,
which showed the desolating effect of the bare
word ; " are we not happy as we are ? Too
happy to run the risk of change ! Frederic,
your ardent imagination will lead you only to
disappointment, and where will be the love to
aid you in sustaining it ? O ! Frederic, remain ;
and, whilst we meet unmolested in these scenes
which you call so exquisite, let us not deserve
to forfeit our lot by growing discontented."

Frederic had wound himself up to such a
pitch of determination to do wonders, that he
was proof against all discouragement ; spoke
 n the proud language of a superior of the accidental advantages of birth and fortune, and
asked where would have been the memory of
the worldly great, had it not been handed down
by the more sublime nobility of genius. The
course of those who travelled amongst the stars

could not be calculated by the dull progress of the wingless being that never soared from earth —a single year, a magic hour, might build him a monument in the waste of ages. "This," continued the excited young German, "is the contemplation to which I would bring my Teresina. These are the daring pinions on which her thoughts must lead me, and let her never doubt that the spirit which she has kindled will closely follow."

Teresina answered with a glow of Roman pride. "If I doubt your genius, Frederic, for what is it that I love you? No; it is the genius to estimate it which I doubt. You think me devoid of courage, but where, in the world's degenerate perception of superiority, are the materials for hope? If they but existed, the soul of the poor girl of Rome would afford them room as readily as that endless waste of ruins could again give space to the heroes who made its history. Oh, could I be tried! Were my courage to be proved by endurance, by sacrifice!"

The dreams of genius were too strong for the arguments of reason. The plaintive beauty of the scene, of the association, and, above all, of the forlorn Teresina, were insufficient to seduce the determined spirit of her lover. They parted with all the grief of a first parting, the one borne up by a daring confidence in the future, the other sinking beneath the discouraging aspect of the present.

Months passed, but the serene absence of positive sorrow existed for Teresina no longer. The scenes of beauty wherein she might have waned away her life in tranquillity had, every one of them, some memorial of a bliss which she had only enjoyed to be sensible of its loss. The melancholy which had characterized her formerly was now an expression of care. The simple occupations which had dimpled the dull placidity of a life devoid of purpose were forgotten in an interest which interfered no otherwise with her state, than by adding to the monotonous a sensation of aching intensity.

From Frederic she had heard, and expected to hear, nothing. In the height of his rash confidence, he had declared that she should hear from him no more till he was thought worthy to obtain her; and a certain degree of morbid and pertinacious pride was likely to keep him to his word. In the slender society which was open to her, and in which she was thrown but rarely, his name indeed was sometimes mentioned amongst others of his profession, but little transpired to cheer her. It was said that there were more professors than patrons, that interest was more needful than talent, and that the triumphs of art had ceased for centuries. She listened with the endurance she had boasted, but her heart was not the less wrung with the picture of his failure, the decline of his self-estimation, the wounded pride which might cause him to abjure her sight for ever. Oh for some project to snatch them both from the exposure to this anguish!——Oh for any sacrifice of herself to save that spirit from the humiliation to which it was destined !

Shortly before this period, circumstances had, for a season, called her lofty relation, the Marchese, to Rome, for the first time since she had grown up. He was a nobleman of high character, and, though far advanced in life, retained a kindliness of feeling which, in other days, had made a stately person and gifted intellect the objects of love, no less than admiration. The mind and beauty of Teresina were of a quality unlooked-for; her parents had been long dead; and the connexions who had succeeded to the charge of her were of a degree so distant as to be scarcely traceable. Her case was touching, and he decided that something must be done for her.

The more the Marchese conversed with her, the more he had cause to wonder at the work of nature which, to appearance, had superseded all necessity for the cultivation which had been denied to her — the more he was attracted by the noble blood which displayed itself in every thought she uttered. Her heart palpitated at each advance of favour, as an omen of good fortune to her Frederic. For the first time in her life, her efforts to confer pleasure, to obtain the influence of affection, were founded in a double interest. The Marchese had not entirely forgotten the gallantry of his youth, was a ready example that the old, as well as the young, are not insensible to the flattery of attention, and began to call to mind that he had paid his late Marchesa the respect of remaining long a widower.

The unexpected turn which had been taken by her noble relative's regard was appalling. Teresina shuddered —such a union could never be.

The keen glance of the Marchese saw more in that maiden confusion than Teresina had expressed. " I am not surprised," he said, with the calm and dignified kindness which resulted from a long acquaintance with human feelings, and a benevolent conviction of the allowance to be made for them—" I am not surprised, that the proposal of a union between elements so opposite as youth and age should, at the first view, be somewhat startling ; but let me not alarm you, if I say that I perceive other objections in that shrinking expression, perhaps, more powerful even than the disparity of years. I do not inquire the secrets of a heart where all is purity, and where it is needless to inflict the pain of distressing. confessions. It is enough for me to know that your affections have not been slumbering, and, indeed, with a disposition like your's, I can hardly be surprised at such a circumstance : but I grieve for its existence. The obscurity of the life which you have passed has rendered it impossible that you can have made any acquaintance suitable to your birth, or, indeed, beyond the humble society of which, to my shame, you have so long formed a part. A marriage that is not noble must never be the fate of Teresina."

Teresina sank beneath the agony of her feelings and hid her face at his feet.

"My fair young kinswoman," he continued, with a struggle between commiseration and pride, "will see the necessity of sacrificing any plebeian partiality, when the honour of our house obliges me to use my influence that no unworthy connexion shall be sanctioned by the church. In addition to this, let me recommend the consideration, Teresina, that I am an old man, and little likely to be a burthen upon my large estates beyond the endurance of your patience, and that at my death there is no heir to dispute your right to them. You will still, in all human probability, be in the bloom of youth and beauty, and may have a long life before you to dispense happiness as you please, and breathe an atmosphere of blessings. Do not give me your answer yet—you are not in a state to reflect. I will leave you to compose yourself, and renew our conversation to-morrow."

Long after he had departed, Teresina remained gazing on the splendours of the pictured wall and fretted ceiling of that stately apartment in anguish and stupefaction. The words which had struck most fearfully upon her heart were those which denied to her hopes the sanction of the church. Frederic had no nobility but his mind. He was lost to her for ever.

The mind of Teresina, however, was not so supinely at the mercy of her affections but that, after they had been relieved of their first wild burst of misery, it could settle down to a firm survey of her position. The simple being of a few months since, who never thought, because there was nothing in her life which called for it, was now driven to weigh the relative importance of events which were to direct her fate, and was to form a judgment which would have been embarrassing to others of her years, whatever might have been their superior advantages. She was offered a connexion against which her nature would have rebelled, even had her heart

not been pre-occupied. She was offered wealth,
which her long habits of self-denial had rendered superfluous. The temptations of society,
so dazzling to young minds generally, were to
her's no temptations at all, for it had been
formed in solitude, and was fixed on contem-
plations far different. To what end, therefore, was she to accede to the wishes of the
Marchese, even though her marriage with Frederic were rendered impossible ? There *was* an
end, nevertheless, of paramount importance to
be answered, which was the conversion of this
impossibility into a matter most feasible. She
had heard it said that the estates of the Marchese
had, in common with a few others, the virtue
of conferring nobility on their possessor. The
train of thought which followed upon this recollection may be imagined. The Marchese had
given his word that they should be her's, and,
by transferring them to Frederic, she placed him
beyond the threat which had dismayed her.

Before the interview of the next day, she
had satisfied herself of the correctness of her
information. She was pale and frozen as any
beautiful creation in the marble around her ;

but she kept in mind that the sacrifice for which she was prepared was for Frederic, and felt that she could unshrinkingly have awaited the stroke of death.

It was not long ere the gems of genius and taste, and the gorgeous devices of wealth, that were squandered through that enchanted palace, gleamed with the glow of festive lights that seemed to outnumber the stars. From quaint balustrade and vaulting statue, the breeze of the early autumn was cooled by fantastic wreaths from fountains of magic source. Tier over tier of myrtle terraces displayed the proud concourse of Rome's loveliest and loftiest born; and the waving bed of odours that melted downward into the dark blue city bore with it the sweetest sounds of joy and melody. There were homage, praise, congratulation—all words for soothing, flattering, and forgetfulness; there were earth's choicest treasures for the adornment of beauty, and heaven's fairest favours to disarm comparison. Alas! and what were all these to the envied of that night — the aching, the bewildered, the *Marchesa* Teresina? In the confusion of her throbbing brain there

was but one object visible—one fearful thought
defined—" Frederic ! Could his form but now
appear amidst this throng, what human protestations could convince him that I am faithful
still ? "

This was the last, as it was the first, moment
of her married life which was willingly devoted
to the remembrance of her lover. She had
taken a desperate step for him, the result remained with Providence, and the intervening
time was to be claimed by the duties of her
new state. With these the thought of Frederic
was incompatible. She dared not dwell upon
the joy it had been in the midst of her desola-
tion. It must be banished ; and, as an indulged
and definite object, it *was* banished. But,
though the shade of fear appeared not, the
apprehension, the tremor, convulsed her still.
Her expression underwent another change. It
was more deathlike, but it was more restless.
It was seeking constantly somewhat that it
dreaded to find. It looked on the spectator
with an appeal for shelter from herself.

The life of a noble lady, in its worldly career,
accorded little with the retiring virtue and

shrinking sensibility of Teresina. Her appearance and youth, when contrasted with the Marchese, could not fail, in such a land as Italy, to surround her with gallantry which was odious and irrepressible. The pattern which she set to the less scrupulous was remarked with ridicule and resented with injury, and, when she received not the mock credit of having found for her husband a feeling new to nature, she was whispered to have at least the merit of constancy and caution in her engagements elsewhere. Such shafts as these, however unmerited, could not drop harmlessly, for the very purity of her bosom only caused a more vivid consciousness of somewhat within it which dared not see the light. Every moment her secret seemed discovered — every throb of her heart was a confession of guilt.

If her situation was painful amongst her equals, before the public it was harrowing. If her splendid equipage passed the streets, her declining head turned not to the right or to the left, from apprehension of *whose* reproachful glance might be fixed upon her. If she knelt for relief before the altar, she dared not raise her

eyes, for fear of *whose* indignant form might in-
terpose.   And when she returned exhausted in
soul to her palazzo, that look, that form, which
first had met her there — which there had
gained dominion of her deepest love — how
could she shun them ? How, except in madness !

The Marchese, who observed with vigilant
kindness every turn of her behaviour, and saw
its motives no less correctly than he had done
at first, became aware that her serenity of mind
was not to be restored by society, or by remaining in a scene of painful associations. She had
never visited his possessions in the mountains,
and his proposal to remove thither was received with an eagerness which showed too
well her piteous yearning for repose. For the
first time, her eyes looked back over the desolate
Campagna, upon the sinking domes and towers
of her native city. If she sighed, it was to
think that it contained no joy, no thing that
she regretted, and that her business was to let
it fade from her memory as it did from her
sight.

When the declining sun shone red upon her

mountain path, there was nothing to remind
her of her scene of trials but the summit of
Soracte, which had formed the loftiest point of
her wondering view, and which now lay behind
her, and a backward gleam of the Tiber winding, like a stream of fire, through the distant
plain, as though to bear her last farewell.

At length the crags of the Apennine, with
their tortuous stems and naked roots of golden
chesnut, their deep bronze clumps of imper-
vious ilex, their crimson arbutus, and all their
nameless hues of autumnal foliage, closed up
the last outlet to a world beyond them. The
ancient castellated chateau crowned a steep
summit, that shot up from forests bounded only
by mountains without end. The boar and the
buck, it would have seemed, might have dwelt
there for ever undisturbed by the foot of man,
had not a few scattered columns of smoke
ascended from the now grey valley, to indicate
the burning of the leaves for purposes of hus-
bandry. The last blaze of the sun likewise,
which caught a few of the loftiest points, was
refracted in one direction by some glittering
white monastery ; in another, by some lonely

penitential cell.   To those who must suffer in
secret, it is a consolation to suffer in solitude,
and already she felt her heart relieved as from
bonds that would not suffer it to swell with its
griefs.

The difference in every thing around, from
her previous mode of life, was perhaps the
source of her ability to exist on.   The spacious
halls, instead of the rich Corinthian sculpture
she had left, brought recollections only of the
rude Goth, the feudal warrior, and the hunter
of the boar.   For statue and picture there
were the piled implements of the chase, and
the carved oaken panel; for the light balcony
there was the deep sombre recess.   The re-
tainers had a bold romantic bearing, like the
mountains that bred them, and the polished
Marchese of the capital was converted into the
more noble chieftain of the wilds.   The beautiful and the elegant had become the awful and
the sublime, and all things harmonized with her
days of sacrifice, as though to aid her through
them.

The Marchese had been all his life an enthusiast of the chase, and the chief events in

Teresina's history were to see him go forth with his troop of mules and motley rangers in the morning, and return with the savage victims of their toils at sunset. Between whiles she would mark the round of the sun, till each fragment of the hills frowned the tardy progress of time with the truth of the dial; and, if her pulse did not stop in despair at the long and heavy journey in advance, it was from the unmurmuring reflection that there was so much the more space to atone for imperfect duty. Sometimes she stood before the rude, den-like habitation of the hunter contadino, with its poverty displayed in the scanty festoons of Indian corn that hung drying from the eves, and the approach in nature between its masters and the animals that supplied their food in the equal participation of its shelter. If an unguarded sigh escaped her that she had not been born even here, she sought comfort in the remembrance that she could not then have endowed it with the happiness she might envy. At other times, she would lose herself in the mysteries of an ancient library ; and, when the conviction flashed upon her that she was amassing lore

c 2

more suitable to her *future* years, she might
perhaps hold herself excused in the consideration that it was fitted to the present ones of
her husband. If any thing of more moment
occurred than this diurnal routine, it was the
ravage of the storm or the daring irruption of
the brigand.

Once or twice, indeed, there were occurrences
which touched her more nearly, and these were
the accidental arrivals of wandering artists, who
were tempted thither by the glowing colours
and savage outline of the landscape. What
made these strangers more painfully interesting was that they were chiefly Germans, for
there is perhaps no nation that pursues its art
with a passion so unremitting.

Happy was the fortune of the poor wayfarer,
which brought him to the home of Teresina.
His wants were supplied with a thrill of sympathy which met him no where else. His simple ardour for the charms of crag and cataract
was listened to with a deeper interest than had
been bestowed upon the proudest in the land,
and his pencil was bespoke for every scene that
could give scope to its genius. The coldest

virtue might find pity for the hidden and scarce acknowledged cause of this distinction; for never did her heart take leave of her prescribed line of duty to drop a word that might obtain the unknown history of Frederic.

In this seclusion, and in these watchful endeavours to direct a suffering heart in a blameless course, were consumed two years. They were years of hard schooling, and did not pass unprofitably. Her mind had attained a higher cast, was stored with knowledge which nothing but such a state of existence might have surmounted, and matured in powers of reflection to a degree that was visible in the more intense character of her beauty. It was the will of Fate that these qualities should now become free to form her well deserved happiness.

Time had dealt kindly with the Marchese, and did not seek his due till the claim was fairly allowed. The old noble forgot not, now that he was about to part from Teresina, the promises he had made before their union. His estates, without exception, were given to her absolute disposal; her praises were the last words on his lips; and when she again saw

Rome, it was in the pompous train which conveyed him to the tomb of his fathers.

Once more a sojourner in the palazzo, the
tumult of her heart so long repressed was hard
indeed to be resisted; but her duty was not
complete till the memory of the Marchese had
received its tribute of respect eqivalent to the
fidelity which she had shown him living.   Ere
her tongue was trusted with the name of
Frederic, the splendid Marchesa had declined
every envied alliance that could be offered by
the Roman nobility, and curiosity was eagerly
attending the end to which her paramount attractions would be devoted.   The humiliation
of her princely suitors was in due time completed by a tremulous inquiry for the obscure
German student; wild were the apprehensions,
the impatience, with which she awaited the result.   Frederic might have forgotten her, might
never have returned to Rome after her marriage, might have believed her false, might no
longer exist.   When her messenger returned,
she was found dishevelled with agitation, and
scarcely able to speak or to comprehend.

Frederic had returned immediately upon

hearing that she was lost to him, had given up the pursuit of fame, and was contented to labour for his bread.

"But comes he not to see me?"

He had sent his humble respects to the noble Marchesa, and would attend her commands when released from work.

"He does not fly to meet me! His humble respects to Teresina!"

Hours passed, and still the trembling mistress of that glittering saloon was doomed to hide her face in the silken cushion with anticipations of woe unknown to the bed of straw. The Madonna breathing from the walls seemed to whisper that the place for hope was not there, and the twilight of the same season that witnessed her sacrifice to the Marchese was a memorial of bitter omen. It was then that the slow opening of the massive door prepared her to learn her fate; was it the door of paradise or the tomb? One hand flung back the dark loose braids from her sight, the other pressed the heart that would have burst. She knew not whether to spring to his arms, or, like a guilty thing, to sink at his feet. The door was closed; and Frederic, in the simple costume of other days, pale, care-worn, but with an aspect more proud than ever, stood before her, alone and calmly.

"Frederic! do you not know me?"

"I know, Signora, that I wait the pleasure of the noblest lady in Rome."

"Frederic, 'tis Teresina—unchanged—with every obstacle to happiness removed, except what you may create yourself. These walls, with all their treasures—mountains and valleys for a dukedom—nobility that may look down upon the proud—power that may raise the crushed hearts of indigence and virtue—these, with the first, pray heaven, the only, object of your love—these all are your's—if you indeed are Frederic, and can at length remember Teresina."

The effort was exhausting—she dropped where she had been reclining, and regarded him with the tremor of a supplicant.

Frederic stood unmoved. "I did not think," he replied, "that it lay in the course of human events to place me under the obligations which I owe to the Marchesa Teresina. I thought that the once aspiring spirit had been crushed to a level with its fortunes——that he who had dropped disheartened on the road to fame would find nothing to break his fall to disgrace. I thought I could have borne insult, have received charity. Thanks to the Marchesa, I see a depth to which I cannot fall. This is indeed a noble palazzo. Here are the works which raised a race of mortals to something between mankind and the gods, and here are powers of enjoyment as far beyond the level of earthly experience. There is a beautiful and gentle phantom of remembrance which used to listen to the transport with which my soul drank in these wonders, and might bear me witness that I knew their worth unequalled. I know besides those mountain domains, and the greatness they bestow. They are endeared to me by the humble transcripts of my fellow labourers. Their possessor might build himself a throne of blessings. But the poor German is not so basely poor, that he can receive even these from a hand polluted——from a heart foresworn."

Teresina could answer only by a low scream of agony.

" That hand," he calmly continued, " without its gifts, had led me perchance upon a course more lofty than that which it paves with gold.   But confidence is the quality of love, and Teresina's heart misgave her.   To what end, therefore, was she to run a perilous hazard, with all that woman looks for at her feet ?   She had her choice, and took the fortune she preferred. The feeling which withheld her not *then* can surely not detract from her enjoyment *now*—and it were hard indeed to sully such a lot by linking it with that which could not soar from the dust."

" Frederic, would you have me die in your presence ?   For what was this mighty lot embraced, unless to make it your's ?—unless to smoothe away impossibilities to my being your's without it ?   Frederic, what has supported me through my bitter trial?—what has restrained the lonely anguish of my heart from seeking sympathy in your's ?—what has made your name a stranger to my lips, your fortunes a mystery, your fate a frightful presentiment, a hovering shadow, which I dared not contemplate and could not banish ? What but the dread of not deserving, of being worthless to you ? Oh ! would you look less calmly, coldly, sternly, I would explain the past so that you should love me better than before we parted. You knew that I was poor, neglected, desponding. I have not words as others have to take my own part. Frederic, will your heart not help me ? I never thought my feeble mind a match for your's, but you pursuaded, you over-rated me, and leave me now to feel it and to perish. Had you not said you loved me, I never had given this palsied hand to the fetters which have poisoned it. I should have lived as you first found me—my harmless history had died with me unstained ; and now my very grave must be my shame, branded with falsehood, and by *you!*''

" Forgive me, Signora—I was ignorant of the fashion of your rank. I did not know it was a proof of constancy to give your hand in opposition to your vows, or a proof of love to break the spirit that bowed to your dominion ; I did not know it was a reproach to call such things by the name of falsehood, and will in future think them virtues which the lowlier born are too vile to comprehend. You will pardon me, for the mistake has cost me dearly. I too was happy when we met, but, in good truth, I have not been since so deserving of a continuance of that condition as the Marchesa Teresina. I have not shown my truth by plighting my faith to any other, by *making her name a stranger to my lips, and her fortunes a mystery.* No, she has been the theme of prayer to the heart she broke—the single thought of the sleepless night and wasted day — the only vision which these eyes have pursued till my brain grew giddy, and this withered brow received, as may be seen, the stamp of the Marchesa's *virtues.* It were preposterous to place two beings of such opposite natures in the same yoke, and I must think that you are merely pleased to amuse a vacant hour, by seeing how far the some time enthusiast continues to be a theme for mockery."

Teresina answered not. She saw in the determined expression of Frederic that protestations were useless, and her look changed to the chill apathy of despair. Frederic could not but be aware that her wound was deep, but his own had been deadly; and he considered that one who had deserted him for the mere advantages of fortune could be vulnerable no where but in her vanity. Still the bitter words which his ruined affection had addressed to her had recoiled with a stunning force. If she was the scorned Marchesa, she had been the adored Teresina.

"We part," he said, in an altered and melancholy voice, "for the last time, and it will be yet another grief to me to know that I have given you pain. Let me atone for it by beseeching you to forget me—your illustrious station demands it of you — or, if you *will* think of me, let it be only as of one too faithful to the thrilling thought of toiling for his Teresina to be able to profit by the noble generosity of the Marchesa."

He turned to depart, and she withheld him not—his farewell was unheard—and in another moment the ponderous iron doors of the palazzo had closed behind him, as he felt, for ever.

The feelings of Frederic, when his brain had
become sufficiently calm to contemplate what
had passed, were not less cruel and overwhelm-
ing than they had been at the first news of
Teresina's marriage.   Whatever they had been
on that occasion, he had retained the consciousness that the injury which he had received was unmerited.   He had reviewed his
conduct with his heart's approval.   He had
been devoted, he had never inflicted a pang, he
had never committed the outrage of a doubt.
The case was now different.   He had seen
Teresina imploring in vain, protesting her innocence unbelieved, and struck dumb with
anguish.   There was an appearance of truth
in the few impassioned words of her defence,
which seemed beyond the reach of art, and, if
it were *not* art, he had behaved like a monster.
Sometimes he almost overcame the morbid
acuteness of pride, which is said to be so inci-
dental to his country, and was in the act of returning to assure himself that he had not been
guilty of injustice.   His love, which, instead of
being destroyed, had seemed to quicken with
the tortures of its ordeal, threatened to whirl

him back to implore her to forgive and re-construct his nature. Then came the insidious consideration of the aspect which such a measure might assume. He had betrayed no impulse of love to make allowance for her, or even to listen to her—he had been restrained by no suggestion of common humanity from expressions which seemed to cut her to the soul. What then could be supposed to bring him back to her presence, but the more deliberate recollection of the splendours he had rejected? This thought was fatal. Had Teresina been desolate in fortune, as she was in feeling, her happiness had been decided. It now depended upon the line which she might chance to adopt, whilst in ignorance that the balance was still wavering; and that she should desire a repetition of the scene she had undergone was scarcely to be expected.

Three days passed, and Frederic received no message from Teresina to return. He began to offer himself bitter congratulations that he had not done so uninvited. Her suffering, as he at first supposed, could have been nothing but mortification at being rejected by one so humble, and doubtless her unsteady regard for him had now settled down to scorn and hatred. If ever he heard of her again, he persuaded himself it would be by some act of Roman vengeance to punish the pauper's insolence, and tie his tongue from betraying her.

The fourth day came, and with it the means of estimating how far his imagination had done her justice. He had, with a determined effort to concentrate his energies, and hide the torture that had scattered them, resumed his occupation in the studio of which he was the pride, and was cleaving the undulations of beauty from a model of forlorn recollection. Visiters, as usual, came and went, but he neither heard their remarks nor turned to behold them. At length he was startled by an inquiry for his own name, and, turning upon his low scaffold, encountered persons of an official aspect, apparently with some object of importance. He had no sooner acknowledged himself to be the person sought than he was saluted with profuse deference and congratulation as the Marchese di ———— ! The vast estates had been legally transferred to his possession, every particle from the richest palace to the most barren crag, and had conveyed every title and distinction enjoyed by those who had preceded him. The chisel dropped from his hands, and his visage became bloodless.

" And the Marchesa!" he exclaimed; " the Marchesa Teresina ?"

" No longer the Marchesa, of which addition she is divested by the relinquishment of the Marquisate, but the simple Signora Teresina. Some mystery in life, which she has not thought proper to explain, has induced her to withdraw from it; and, to the astonishment and grief of all Rome, she is believed to have retired to the cloister. Her declared motive for the present disposal of what would probably have wedded to the world any other being upon earth, is her desire to leave it to the person most worthy to enjoy it. No other particulars are known, nor the place of her retreat.

This, then, was the anticipated scorn and hatred——this was the Roman vengeance! Teresina had been the only hope, the only joy, the only woe, of his life—she was now life itself. The event of her history, which had stained her with the imputation of baseness and falsehood, had become an unparalleled proof of her courageous truth. The pangs of her sacrifice, the virtues of her endurance, exalted her from a being worthy of all love, to one who commanded his worship. Whither should he fly to cast his contrition at her feet ?—Whither ?—She had renounced the grandeur, which had deceived her hopes, in darkness and solitude ; not a vestige of her remained but the anguish of her absence, and not a clue to arrest the gloomy purpose which must make that absence eternal. In vain did Frederic implore the amazed domestics, and every individual, from the highest to the lowest, with whom she was known to have been acquainted. Equally in vain did he offer benefactions to the priests, rewards to the police, nay, the sacrifice of his entire wealth to the state, for the mere boon of being brought to see her. Weeks elapsed, and Teresina appeared to have vanished from the earth.

The effects upon a heart like that of Frederic

were destroying. To occupy a home which had been vacated for him by the wounded soul of Teresina would have been to lay himself in the grave. As he groaned upon the pallet so long haunted by her image as the proud and exulting deceiver, the now changed aspect of the vision to the subdued melancholy that had once depended on him for every joy of earth was the guise of an accusing spirit, which left him no alternative but escape or madness. He determined to fly from Rome for ever. If at one time he shrank from leaving the land in which she had loved him, at another, he reflected that, though unseen, her eye might be upon him still; and that his rejection of her gifts without her love might induce her to come forth and resume them. His conduct had doubtless so estranged her affection, as to render it impossible that they could ever enjoy them together.

The authorities by whom he had so lately been invested with his greatness were summoned to a second disposition of it; and persons were appointed to hold it in the right of Teresina. He then sought the worthy priest who had acted as her confessor, with a view to leaving his last words, should she ever be found to receive them.

The priest looked upon the haggard countenance of his visiter with interest and compassion. He had much to listen to, the chief part of which was an impassioned recital of the foregoing events, with the feelings and resolution which they had produced.

" Son," said the benevolent old man, " you have doubtless been to blame for judging so rashly from appearances, without admitting so much as a word of explanation from one whom you had reason to believe so pure. A moral might be drawn from it of deep import, but it has brought its punishment, and I am not one to apply bitter truths to a heart that is bleeding. Let me rather counsel you that one mistake of passion may not be followed by another. You are going forth, you know not whither, in a frenzy of desperation, which you believe to be the return of an ardent and disappointed affection. How know you that this is not a mere feeling of remorse for having caused sorrow to one whom you have found to be generous and faithful; and on whom, if found, you would bring greater sorrow than ever, by discovering too late that your love has in reality passed away? Think how much preferable to such a case is the lot which she is supposed to have embraced—the calm devotion to things which know not disappointment. Think, and the consideration may moderate half your affliction."

"Father, your sacred function makes you well acquainted with the traits of remorse, and the griefs that admit of consolation. I have no answer to make but such as your penetrating eye may read. For her—it may be well if she shares your doubts—I would not have the memory of one who has blasted her young days hang heavy on a stainless conscience; and, if it will serve her to think I can forget, it would be a base vengeance to undeceive her. You regard me, father, with a look of deep scrutiny. If any portion of my heart seems unrevealed, declare it, and be satisfied. What is there that the soul so beggared should desire to hide?"

"I was musing," returned the priest, "that

life is uncertain to all men, and that mine can
reckon but a few years at most. It may hereafter be important that all which you have said
should be known, and none may remain to tell.
I would fain ask you to aid an old man's memory
in relating it to ears more likely to retain it.''

So saying, he took the arm of Frederic, and
presently they were passing along the velvet
bank of the Tiber below the city. It was one
of those dark, melancholy, sunless days, which
give to the autumn its richest hues and most
melting sentiment. The fringe of yellow canes
on the opposite side bowed motionless to their
unbroken reflection in the wave; and a few
scattered clumps of crimson foliage slept
against the deep blue distance without a flutter
or a sigh. Not far in front, a few precipitous
heights presented a sombre contrast of brown
monastic building and spiral cypress, whilst
every bell that trembled through the still atmosphere, from the deep St. Peter's to the clank
of the hermit monk, had a tone which carried
that gloom to the heart. Frederic spoke not,
and neither cared nor observed whither they
were going, until they reached a gentle accli-

vity, paved with broad easy steps, over which the grass and a few wild flowers trailed carelessly, to show how little that path was used as a link with the world. The funereal trees which had spoken mournfulness in the distance now reared their slender columns and swelled into shadow on either side; and at every few steps was a crucifix, with some saintly inscription to dispel the memory of scenes less holy.

At the end of this avenue was a sad-looking edifice, with gothic arches and balustraded galleries, with an image of the Holy Virgin beside the ponderous doors, and a broad dial above them, which had no sun to mark the hour, and seemed to indicate a place where time stood still. The priest touched the bell, the latch rose with a string, and they traversed gallery and quadrangle as though the walls were deserted, till they entered an apartment of the interior, where Frederic was left alone.

All that he had observed on his approach was that he was probably conducted to the holy father's monastery; and he gazed from the deep casement on the remote city of sorrows without heeding the moments that passed, or giving a thought to what they might produce. At length the father returned; his face was not free from emotion, and he prepared his companion for the exhortations of one who had experience to appreciate his grief and to direct its cure.

" You have no word to say," continued he; " your tale is told; and your deepest sin absolved by a spirit whose pardon will be ratified."

There was a mystery in the old man's manner, and a tear in his eye, by which Frederic was startled into a sudden perception of the place in which he stood. His agitation increased to a shudder.

" Father," he exclaimed, " what place is this? This is no house of holy brotherhood. These flowers—these delicate works of charity —these implements of woman's occupation— bear witness all to the wild whispering of my soul. This is the convent—Teresina the forgiving spirit!—Deny it, and forgiveness comes too late ! "

He flung himself in frenzy at the confessor's feet; and, as he gasped for speech, a hand

placed gently on his head bestowed its blessing—a voice of melody from the spheres pronounced the name of Frederic—and at the
same moment his arms received his Teresina.

THE LOVER'S QUARREL.

A TALE OF THE ENGLISH CHRONICLES.

Alas, how light a cause may move
Dissension between hearts that love !
Hearts that the world in vain had tried,
And sorrow but more closely tied ;
That stood the storm when waves were rough,
Yet in a sunny hour fell off,
Like ships that have gone down at sea
When heaven was all tranquillity.

Moore.

I WISH I could describe the young Lady Sibyl :
she was rather tall than otherwise, and her
head was carried with a toss of the prettiest
pride I ever saw ; in truth, there was a supernatural grace in her figure, by which she was
in duty bound to be more lofty in her demean-
our than other people. Her eyes were of a
pure, dark hazel, and seemed to wander from
the earth as though they were surprised how
they happened to drop out of the skies ; and
the sweet, high, and mighty witchery that sport-

ed round her threatening lips inspired one with a wonderful disposition to fall down and worship her. It was, of course, not to be expected that such a strangely gifted lady should be quite so easily contented with her cavaliers as those who were not gifted at all ; and Sibyl, very properly, allowed it to be understood that she despised the whole race. She likewise allowed it to be understood that, the world being by no means good enough for her, she conceived the best society it afforded to be her own wilful cogitations ; and that she meant to pass the whole of her pretty life in solitude and meditation. People conjectured that she was in love, and too proud to show it ; and Sibyl surmised that they were vastly impertinent, and by no means worth satisfying.

There was a small grotto by the lake that wound before the old arched windows of the hall ; a world of fine foliage was matted fantastically above and around it, so as to exclude every intruder but the kingfisher, who plunged, meteor-like, on his golden prey, and vanished in the shade before he was well seen ; and an endless variety of woodbines leaped from branch to branch, swinging their dewy tendrils in the air, and showering fragrance upon the green moss beneath, or stealing round the rustic pinnacles, like garlands twined by Cupid for his favourite hiding-place. It was in this choice retreat that the Lady Sibyl chose to forget the world in which she was born, and imagine that for which she seemed created; and in this mood, without manifesting any particular symptoms of exhaustion, excepting that she had grown a little more pale and more slender, she continued for three whole years.

On the third anniversary of her resolution—she knew it was the third, because the said resolution happened to have been made on the same day that her wild cousin, who had earned for himself the title of Childe Wilful, chose for his departure to the wars—on the third anniversary, as on all other days, Sibyl again tripped down the chase to live in paradise till tea-time; but, not as on other days, the noble summer sunset seemed to have stained her cheek with a kindred hue. Ere she reached her wilderness, she looked back again and again at the hall, slackened her pace that it might not appear hurried, and gazed as long upon the swans and water-lilies as though they really occupied her thoughts. Meanwhile, the flower of the fox-hunting chivalry were carousing with her father in the banqueting-room, and flourishing their glasses to her health. The most mighty and censorious dames of the land were seen stalking up and down the terrace, as stately and as stiff as the peacocks clipped out of the yew-trees at either end of it. Sibyl seemed to have lost the faculty of despising them, and was half afraid that her desertion would be thought strange. As she stood irresolute whether to go on or turn back, she was startled by a voice close by, and the blood leaped in a deeper crimson to her cheek.

" Sibyl! dear Sibyl!" it exclaimed, " wilt thou come, or must I fetch thee, before the whole posse of them ?"

Sibyl tossed her head and laughed; and with an agitated look, which was meant to be indifferent, strolled carelessly into the shade, just in time to prevent the intruder from putting his threat in execution. He was a light, well-made cavalier, with black moustaches and ringlets, and a high-born eye and forehead, which could have looked almost as proud as Sibyl's. As for his accomplishments, the fine Frenchified slashing of his costume, and the courageous manner in which he assaulted a lady's hand, bespoke him a wonder.

"And so, my gallant cousin," said Sibyl, with a voice which was a little out of breath, and with a feeble effort to extricate her fingers, "and so you have brought your valour back to besiege my citadel again."

"Sweet arrogance! is it not the day three thousand years on which we parted; and did I not promise to be here at sunset?"

"I believe you threatened me that you would. Pray, have you run away from battle to be as good as your word?"

"And pray, did you always consider it a threat, or did you tell me that this grotto should be your hermitage till my return?"

"And pray, for the third time, do not be inquisitive; and trouble yourself to let go my hand, and sit down on that seat over the way, and tell me what you have been doing these three days."

" I will, as you desire, take both your hands and the other half of your chair, and tell you, as you surmise, that I have been thinking of you till the thought became exceedingly troublesome : and now oblige me by telling me whether you are as proud as ever since you lost your beauty, or whether you have ever mustered humility to drop a tear for the mad blood which I have shed in toiling to be worthy such a mighty lady ? "

Sibyl laughed, and snatched away her hand from him to draw it across her eyes.

" Dear Sibyl," he continued, in a gentler tone, " and has not that wild heart changed in three long years ?——And has not such an age of experience made our boy and girl flirtation a folly to be amended ? And do I find you the same ——excepting far more lovely——the same perverse being who would not have given her wayward prodigal for the most dismally sensible lord of the creation ? Often as I have feared, I have had a little comforter which told me you could not change. See, Sibyl, your miniature half given, half stolen, at our last parting ;——it has been my shield in a dozen fights, has healed, with its smile as many wounds;—it has asked me if this was a brow whereon to register deceit—if these were the lips to speak it—if these were the eyes——as I live, they are weeping even now!"

She did not raise them from her bosom, but answered, with a smile of feigned mortification, that she thought it very impertinent to make such minute observations. "I, too, have had my comforter," she said, drawing the fellow-miniature from her bosom, and holding it playfully before his eyes;—"it has been my shield against a dozen follies—it has warned me to benefit by sad experience;—it has asked if this was the brow whereon to register any thing good—if these were the lips to speak it—if these were the eyes——as I live, they are conceited even now!"

"But have you indeed kept my picture so close to your heart?"

"And do you indeed think that your old rival, Sir Lubin of the Golden Dell, would have given me a farthing for it?"

"Did you ever try him?"

"Oh, Childe Wilful! can you change coun-

tenance at such a name even now? No; I did
not try him, and (for you are a stranger and
must be indulged), I will tell you wherefore.
I would not have given it him for his head;
nor for as many of them as would have built a
tower to yonder moon; and so now see if you
can contrive to be jealous of him;—nay, you
shall not touch it. Do you remember how
often, when it pleased you to be moody, you
threatened to take it from me?"

"No more of that, sweet Sibyl."

"And will you never counterfeit a headache,
to hide your displeasure, when I dance with
Sir Dunce, or gallop with Sir Gosling?"

"No, never, Sibyl."

"And you will never take leave of me for
ever, and return five minutes afterwards to see
how I bear it?"

"Never, whilst I live."

"Why, then, I give you leave to ask my
father's leave to stay a whole week at the hall,
for I have a great deal to say to you—when I
can think of it."

"I will ask him for yourself, Sybil."

"No, no, Sir Childe, you will not do any

such thing. When you went from hence, it was with a college character, which was by no means likely to ingratiate you with reasonable people, whatever it may have done with other folks ; and you must not talk to my father of the treasured Sibyl till you are better acquainted with him. Talk of ploughs and politics as much as you please;——make it appear that, now the wars are over, there is some chance of your turning your sword into a pruning hook, and yourself into an accomplished 'squire ;—— and then——and then, alas! for the high-minded Sibyl!"

*   *   *   *

It was not long afterwards that Childe Wilful, to the great surprise of Sibyl, arrived at the hall in hot haste from foreign parts! He had always been a favourite for his liveliness, and was, indeed, almost as much liked as abused. The old lord took him by the hand, with a comical expression of countenance which seemed to inquire how much mischief he had done; and the old ladies thought him vastly improved by travel, and awfully like a great warrior.

The only persons to whom his presence
was not likely to be strikingly agreeable,
were a few round-shouldered suitors of Sibyl,
who, in common with country squires in general, were largely gifted with the blessings of
fleet horses and tardy wits. Amongst these
stood pre-eminent, Sir Lubin of the Golden
Dell. He was a tall man, with not a bad figure,
and really a handsome face; though the dangerous tendency of the first was somewhat
marred by peculiar ideas of the Graces, and
the latter was perfectly innocuous, from an undue economy of expression. Altogether, Sir
Lubin was a very fine camel : he was a man of
much dignity, always preserving a haughty
silence when he did not exactly know what to
say, and very properly despising those whom
he could not hope to outshine. Thus it was
that the meeting between Sir Lubin and Childe
Wilful was very similar to that between Ulysses
and the ghost of Ajax.

Had this been all the mortification which the
Childe was doomed to undergo, he might perhaps have contrived to bear it with fortitude;
but Sibyl had subjected him to the task of ob-

taining a good character, and his trials were insupportable.

In the first place, he had to tell stories of sacked cities and distressed virgins, at the tea-table, till he became popular enough with the maiden aunts to be three parts out of his mind; for Sibyl was all the time compelled to endure the homage of her other lovers. It is true that her keen wit could no more enter their double-blocked skulls, than the point of her needle could have penetrated the Macedonian phalanx; but then each villain fixed his eye upon her with all the abstracted expression of the bull's eye in a target, and seemed so abominably happy, that the sight was excruciating. Sometimes, too, Sir Lubin would muster brains to perceive that he was giving pain, and would do his best to increase it, by whispering in her ear, with a confidential smile, some terrible nothing, for which he deserved to be exterminated; whilst, to mend the matter, the old ladies would remark upon the elegance of his manner, and hint that Sibyl was evidently coming to, because she seemed too happy to be scornful, and had lost all her taste for solitude. They would undoubtedly make a very handsome couple; and the Childe was appealed to whether he did not think that they would have a very fine family.

In the second place, his opinions of ploughs and politics, on which love had taught him to discourse but too successfully, made him a fixture at the punch-bowl; while Sir Lubin and his tribe profaned Sibyl's hand in country-dances as long as they had breath for a plunge. It, moreover, left them ample opportunity to negotiate with the aunts upon the arrangement of her plans for the next day, when he was still condemned to admire some new farm, or ride ten miles to rejoice with his host over a wonderful prize-bullock. Sometimes, too, the old lord would apologize for taking him away, by observing, that it was better to leave Sibyl to her lovers, for it was time that she should take up with some one of them, and the presence of third parties might abash her.

In the third place, when he retired to bed to sum up all the pleasures of the day, it was never quite clear to him that Sibyl did not expose him to more disquietude than was abso-

lutely necessary. It might indeed be proper
that her attachment to him should not be too
apparent till he was firmly established in grace,
seeing that his merit was the only thing that
could be put in the scale against the finest
glebe in the county; but then could she not
appear sufficiently careless about him without
being so unusually complaisant to such a set
of louts ?——If his presence made her happy,
there was no necessity to give them licence to
presume to be happy likewise; and, besides,
she might surely find *some* moments for revisit-
ing her grotto, instead of uniformly turning
from his hasty whisper, with——" It is better
not." It was not so formerly, and it was very
reasonable to suppose that her three years'
constancy had been sustained by some ideal
picture of what he might turn out, in which
she was now disappointed. He could not
sleep. His restless fancy continually beheld
her bright eyes looking tenderness upon the
wooden face of Sir Lubin. He turned to the
other side, and was haunted by a legion of
young Lubins, who smiled upon him with
Sibyl's looks till he almost groaned aloud. In

the morning he came down with a hag-ridden countenance, which made people wonder what was the matter with him, and Sibyl asked him, with a look of ineffable archness, whether he was experiencing a return of his headaches.

Time rolled on very disagreeably. The Childe grew every day more pale and popular: the old ladies gave him more advice, and the old lord gave him more wine, and Sibyl grew mortified at his mistrust, and Sir Lubin grew afraid of his frown, and one half of the hall could not help being sorry, and the other half were obliged to be civil. Ajax and Ulysses had stepped into each other's shoes, and Sibyl, to keep the peace, was obliged to accede to an interview in her little boudoir.

It was a fine honey-dropping afternoon. The sweet south was murmuring through the lattice amongst the strings of the guitar, and the golden fish were sporting till they almost flung themselves out of their crystal globe : it was just the hour for every thing to be sweet and harmonious—but Sibyl was somewhat vexed and the Childe was somewhat angry. He was much obliged to her for meeting him, but he feared that he was taking her from more agreeable occupations ; and he was, moreover, alarmed lest her other visiters should want some one to amuse them. He merely wished to ask if she had any commands to his family, for whom it was time that he should think of setting out ; and when he had obtained them he would no longer trespass upon her condescension. Sibyl leant her cheek upon her hand, and regarded him patiently till he had done. "My commands," she gravely said, "are of a confidential nature, and I cannot speak them if you sit so far off."

As she tendered her little hand, her features broke through their mock ceremony into a half smile, and there was an enchantment about her which could not be withstood.

"Sibyl," he exclaimed, "why have you taken such pains to torment me ?"

"And why have you so ill attended to the injunctions which I gave you ? "

"Ill !—Heaven and earth ! Have I not laboured to be agreeable till my head is turned topsy-turvy ? "

"Oh, yes ; and hind-side before, as well, for

it is any thing but right. But did I tell you to pursue this laudable work with fuming and frowning, and doubting and desperation, till I was in an agony lest you should die of your exertions, and leave me to wear the willow ?"

The cavalier stated his provocation with much eloquence.

"Dear Sibyl," he continued, "I have passed a sufficient ordeal. If I really possess your love, let me declare mine at once, and send these barbarians about their business."

"Or rather be sent about your own, if you have any; for you cannot suppose that the specimen which you have given of your patient disposition is likely to have told very much in your favour."

"Then why not teach them the presumption of their hopes, and tell them that you despise them ? "

"Because they are my father's friends, and because, whatever their hopes may be, they will probably wait for encouragement before they afford me an opportunity of giving my opinion thereupon."

"But has there been any necessity to give

them so much more of your time—so many more of your smiles—than you have bestowed upon me ? ''

" And is it you who ask me this question ?— Oh !—is it possible to mete out attentions to those we love with the same indifference which we use towards the rest of the world ?—Would nothing, do you think—no tell-tale countenance—no treacherous accent, betray the secret which it is our interest to maintain ? Unkind to make poor Sibyl's pride confess so much ! ''

The cavalier did not know whether he ought to feel quite convinced. He counted the rings upon the fingers, which were still locked in his own, three times over.

" Sibyl,'' he at last said, " I cannot bear them to triumph over me, even in their own bright fancies. If you are sincere with me, let us anticipate the slow events of time—let us seek happiness by the readiest means—and, trust me, if it is difficult to obtain consent to our wishes, you are too dear to despair of pardon for having acted without it.''

" And you would have me fly with you ? ''

Sibyl shrank from the idea;—her pride was no longer assumed in sport. "You do well," she resumed, "to reproach me with the duplicity which I have practised. It is but just to suppose that she who has gone so far would not scruple to make the love which has been lavished upon her the inducement for her disobedience; that the pride which has yielded so much would be content to be pursued as a fugitive, and to return as a penitent."

"Then, Sibyl, you do not love me?"

"I am not used to make assurances of that kind, any more than I am inclined to submit to the charge of deceit."

"Methinks, Lady Sibyl," he replied, with somewhat of bitterness, "you very easily take offence to-night. It certainly is better to be free from one engagement before we enter upon another."

Sibyl's heart beat high, but she did not speak.

"It is possible that you may have mistaken your reasons for enjoining me to silence; for it is, no doubt, advisable that your more eligible friends should have the opportunity of speaking first.''

Sibyl's heart beat higher, and the tears sprang to her eyes, but her head was turned away.

'' We have staid too long,'' she said with an effort at composure.

'' I thank you, Lady Sibyl,'' he replied, rising haughtily to depart, '' for allowing me to come to a right understanding.   And now——''

Her anger had never been more than a flash, —she could hardly believe him serious, and if he was, he would soon repent.

'' And now,'' she interrupted him, relapsing into her loveliest look of raillery, '' Childe Wilful would be glad of his picture again ?''

'' You certainly will oblige me by restoring it.''

'' Why do you not ask Sir Lubin for it ? ''

'' Lady Sibyl, I am serious ; and I must beg to remark that it can be but an unworthy satisfaction to retain it for a boast to your new lovers.''

'' I do not see that there is any thing to

boast of in it. The face is not a particularly handsome one, and as for him for whom it is meant, he has never made a figure in any history, excepting his own letters. Here is one in my dressing-case—I pray you stand still now while I read over the wondrous exploits which you performed in your last battle, for I think you must have looked just as you do now."

There is no saying whether his resolution would have been firm enough to persist in his dire demand, had not the Lady Sibyl's attendant at that moment entered with Sir Lubin's compliments, and it was past the hour at which she had engaged to ride with him. Childe Wilful's heart was armed with a thicker coat of mail than ever, and his lips writhed into a bitter smile.

" Do not let me detain you, Lady Sibyl," he said ; " perhaps your gentlewoman will be good enough to find me the picture amongst your cast-off ornaments."

This was rather too much—to be exposed in her weakest point to the impertinent surprise of her servant.

"Nay—nay," she replied in confusion, "have done for the present; if you ask me for it to-morrow I will return it."

"I shall not be here to-morrow, and it is hardly compatible with the Lady Sibyl's pride to retain presents which the donor would resume."

Her answer was a little indignant—his rejoinder was a little more provoking—the maid began to laugh in her sleeve—and Sibyl felt herself humiliated. It is but a short step, in mighty spirits, from humiliation to discord; and Sibyl soon called in the whole force of her dignity, and conjured up a smile of as much asperity as the Childe's.

"No!" she exclaimed, "it is not amongst my cast-off ornaments. I mistook it for the similitude of true affection, of generosity and manliness, and have worn it where those qualities deserve to be treasured up."

The picture was produced from its pretty hiding-place and carelessly tendered to him.

"You will, perhaps, remember," she continued, "that there was a fellow to this picture, and that the original of it has as little in-

clination as other people to be made a boast
of.''

"Undoubtedly, Lady Sibyl—it was my intention to make you perfectly easy on that
point.''

The little jewel was removed coldly from his
breast, and seemed to reproach him as it parted,
for it had the same mournful smile with which
Sibyl had sat for it when he was preparing for
the wars. He gave it to her, and received his
own in return. It was yet warm from its sweet
depository, and the touch of it thrilled to his
soul;—but he was determined for once to act
with consistency. As he closed the door he
distinguished a faint sob, and a feeling of self-
reproach seemed fast coming over him; but
then his honour!—was he to endure the possibility of being triumphed over by such an
eternal blockhead as Sir Lubin of the Golden
Dell?

Sibyl made her appearance in the drawing-
room, soon after him, in her riding-dress. Her
manner was cold and distant, and she heard
him feign business at home without condescending to notice it, only there was a fever

upon her cheek, which spoke an unwonted
tumult of feeling.   Her horse was at the door,
and Sir Lubin was ready to escort her down.
As she took leave of her cousin they were both
haughty, and both their hands trembled.   In a
minute she was seen winding through the old
avenue.   Sir Lubin, who was observed poking
his head from his shoulders with all the grace
of a goose in a basket, was evidently saying
tender things, and, altogether, looked cruelly
like a dangerous rival.   The Childe drew his
breath through his teeth as though they had
been set on edge, and moved from the window
like a spirit turned out of Paradise.

Sir Lubin did not find his ride very satisfactory.   He discovered that it was a fine evening ;——made a clever simile about Lady Sibyl's
cheek and a poppy——and another about her
cruelty and a bramble ; but they had little or
no effect.   She answered " no" when she ought
to have said " yes," looked bewildered when he
asked her opinion, and, in fact, as he poetically
expressed it, was extracting honey from the
flowers of her own imagination.

" Will he indeed have the heart to leave me

thus ? " said Sibyl to herself. " Unkind—un-
grateful—to take my little treasure from me—
the sole companion of my bosom—the witness
of all the tears I have shed for him—the comforter of all my doubts of his fidelity ;—it is
gone for .ever—I never can stoop to receive it
back,—I never will forgive him—no, never—
that is, if he be really gone."

And really, when she returned, he *was* gone.
Sibyl, however, would not persuade herself
that it was not his intention to return ; and
every night had to take her pride to task for
having looked out upon the road all the day.
Perhaps he would write ; and she stole away
as heretofore, alone, to meet the tardy post a
mile off. There were letters for my lord—for
Sir Lubin—for the Lady Jemima.

" No—no !—I want not them. For the Lady
Sibyl—what for the Lady Sibyl ? "

The letters were turned over and over, and
still the same deadening sound fell like a knell
upon her heart—" Nothing for the Lady Sibyl."

She returned unwillingly to her company, and
retired, at the first opportunity, to wonder if
her cousin were really in earnest—if he had

really deserted her, and whether she had ever given him cause to do so. Her pride would seldom suffer her to weep, and the tears seemed swelling at her heart till each throb was a throb of pain. Sometimes she would bewilder herself with suggesting other reasons than want of inclination for his absence, and for his silence. Might he not wish to return, and be prevented by his family, who had not seen him for so long, and would naturally be importunate? Might he not be fearful of writing, lest his letter should fall into hands for which it was not intended, and betray the secret which she had desired him to keep? It surely might be her own overweening caution that was afflicting her, and he might be as impatient as herself. Her imagination would begin to occupy itself in ideal scenes, till she forgot those which had really occurred, and her hand would rise fondly to her bosom to draw forth the semblance of her suffering cavalier. Alas! it was then that poor Sibyl's deceptive dreams were dispersed. The picture was gone—was even now, perhaps, the bosom companion of another, who pitied her with smiles, and gaily upbraided him for his falsehood. Then again would the flush of shame rush over her cheek, her maiden indignation determine to forget him, and her wildered wits busy themselves upon plans of teaching him that she had done so.

In the mean time Sir Lubin began to congratulate himself that he had made an impression. Sibyl had lost the spirit to repel his advances as she had done before, and the little she had afforded him of her company was clearly a pretty stratagem to bring him to an explanation. He had a great mind to be cruel in his turn, and lead her heart the dance, as he expressed it, which she had led his—but then she was very pale, and might have a fit of illness. On the evening when he had resolved to make her happy, Sibyl indeed received a letter, but it was from her lover's sister. It was full of the gay rattle which usually characterizes the correspondence of hearts which have never known sorrow; but it was other news that Sibyl looked for. She toiled through lively descriptions of fêtes, and finery, and flirtations, scarcely knowing what she read, till, at last, her eyes glanced upon the name she sought.

E 2

She stopped to breathe ere she proceeded, and then, Childe Wilful was gone to —————, and was paying violent attention to the Lady Blanche.

She tore the letter calmly into little strips;—her lips were compressed with beautiful, but stern and desperate determination. That night Sir Lubin made his proposals, and, in the delirium of fancied vengeance, Sibyl answered—she knew not what.

It was not long after that the Childe was returning sadly home from the Lady Blanche. She was very beautiful—but, oh, she had not the speaking glance of Sibyl. She was lofty and high-minded; but it was not the sweet pride that fascinated whilst it awed—it was the aspiring woman, and not the playful and condescending seraph. She was accomplished; but they were the accomplishments approved by the understanding rather than the heart—the methodical work of education, and stored up for display. But Sibyl was accomplished by heaven! her gifts were like the summer breezes which sported about him—wild, exquisite, and mysterious—which were the same, whether wasted on the desert, or wafting delight to the multitude.   She was a lovely line of poetry in a world of prose—she was a blossom dropped from Paradise to shame all the flowers of the earth.   Oh, but Sibyl was false ! and oh, again, it was just possible that he might be mistaken.   He was sadly bewildered, had another bad headache, and was strongly of opinion that it was not the way to forget Sibyl to put her in competition with other people.   He hardly liked to confess it to himself, but he was not quite sure that, if he had any excuse which would not compromise his dignity, he would not turn his horse's head towards the hall, and suffer the fiends which were tormenting him to drive him at their own pace.

It happened that such excuse was not far distant.   He had no sooner alighted at home than he was presented with a hasty note, which had been for some days awaiting him, from Sibyl's father, inviting him—a film came over his eyes, and the pulsation of his heart was paralyzed—inviting him to what he knew would give him great pleasure, to Sibyl's wedding !   Should he send an excuse, and stay at home, and prove that he did not care about it ; or should he plunge headlong into their revelry, and spare neither age nor sex of the whole party ? No matter, he would consider of it on his way. He gave his steed the spur as though the good animal had been Sir Lubin himself, and set out to cool his blood, and shake his wits into their places, by a moonlight gallop of a hundred miles.

The morning was far advanced when he came within sight of the hall. He was almost exhausted; and the preparations for festivity, upon the fine slope of the chase, came over his soul with sickness and dismay. The high blood of his poor animal was barely sufficient to answer the feeble urging of its rider; and the slow stride, which was accompanied by a deeper and a deeper sob, seemed fast flagging to a stand still. The Childe felt that he was too late. He inquired of a troop of merry-makers round a roasting ox, and found that the wedding cavalcade had set off for the church. He looked down upon the hilt of his sword —he was still in time for vengeance—still in time to cut short the bridegroom's triumph—to disappoint the anticipations of —— Spirits of fury ! were there none to inspire a few minutes' vigour into his fainting steed. The steed toiled on as though he had possessed the burning heart of his master ;—troops of peasant girls, dressed fantastically, and waving garlands on either side of the road, soon told him that he was near the scene of the sacrifice. They had received a sheep-faced duck from the head of the blushing Sir Lubin—a sprawling wave of his long arm, thrust, in all the pride of silver and satin, from the window of his coach and six. They had beheld the fevered and bewildered loveliness of the Lady Sibyl, looking, amongst her bridemaids, intense as a planet amidst its satellites, and they were all in ecstasies, which, if possible, increased his agony. Another lash, another bound, and he turned the corner which brought him full upon the old elm-embowered church, surrounded by the main body of the May-day multitude, and a string of coaches which displayed all the arms in the county. He sprang from his horse, and dashed through them like a meteor. The party was still standing before the altar ; and he staggered and restrained his steps to hear how far the ceremony had proceeded. There was a dead silence, and all eyes were fixed upon Sibyl, who trembled, as it seemed, too much to articulate.

"More water," said one in a low voice; "she is going to faint again."

Water was handed to her, and the clergyman repeated—"Wilt thou take this man for thy wedded husband?"

Sibyl said nothing, but gasped audibly; her father looked more troubled, and Sir Lubin opened his mouth wider and wider.

The question was repeated, but still Sibyl spoke not.

It was pronounced a third time — Sibyl shook more violently, and uttered an hysteric scream.

"Oh, merciful Heaven!" she exclaimed, "it is impossible!—I cannot!—I cannot!"

Her astonished lover sprang forward, and received her fainting form in his arms. A glance at each other's countenance was sufficient to explain all their sufferings—to dissipate all their resentment. Concealment was now out of the question, and their words broke forth at the same instant.

" Oh, faithless! how could you drive me to this dreadful extremity ?"

" Sweet Sibyl, forgive—forgive me ! I will atone for it by such penitence, such devotion, as the world never saw."

" By Jove !" exclaimed the bridegroom, " but I do not like this !"

" By my word !" added the Lady Jemima, " but here is a new lover !"

" By mine honour !" responded the Lady Bridget, " but he is an old one !"

" By my word and honour too !" continued the lady something else, " I suspected it long ago !"

" And by my grey beard," concluded the old lord, " I wish I had done so too !—Look you, Sir Lubin, Sibyl is my only child, and must be made happy her own way. I really thought she had been pining and dying for you, but since it appears I was mistaken, why e'en let us make the best of it. You can be brideman still, though you cannot be bridegroom; and

E 5

who knows but in our revels to-night, you may
find a lady less liable to change her mind ? "

Sir Lubin did not understand this mode of
proceeding, and would have come to high
words but for the peculiar expression of Childe
Wilful's eye, which kept them bubbling in his
throat. He could by no means decide upon
what to say. He gave two or three pretty
considerable hems, but he cleared the road in
vain, for nothing was coming; and so, at last,
he made up his mind to treat the matter with
silent contempt. He bowed to the company
with a haughty dive, kicked his long sword, as
he turned, between his legs, and strode, or
rather rode, out of the church as fast as his
dignity would permit. The crowd on the out-
side, not being aware of what had passed within,
and taking it for granted that it was all right
that the bridegroom, on such great occasions,
should go home alone, wished him joy very
heartily and clamorously, and the six horses
went off at a long trot, which was quite grand.

Sibyl and her cavalier looked breathlessly for
what was to come next.

" The wedding feast must not be lost," said the old lord ; " will nobody be married ? "

Sibyl was again placed at the altar, and, in the room of Sir Lubin, was handed the Cavalier Wilful.

" Wilt thou take *this* man for thy wedded husband ? " demanded the priest.

Sibyl blushed, and still trembled, but her faintings did not return ; and if her voice was low when she spoke the words " I will," it was distinct and musical as the clearest note of the nightingale.

FAITHFUL AND FORSAKEN.

A Dramatic Sketch.

PERSONS.

EUSTACHE.

MERZON.

GERAULT.

OFFICERS, GENS-D'ARMES, &c.

ANNABELLE.

MARGUERITE.

PEASANTRY, &c.

FAITHFUL AND FORSAKEN.

PART I.

SCENE—*The Country near Paris—Evening.*—ANNA-
BELLE, MARGUERITE; *Peasant Girls, &c. dropping
off by degrees.*

ANNABELLE, *(taking* MARGUERITE *by the hand)*.
LIGHT-HEARTED France, whose deepest groans are
      breathed
To merry pipes and mirth-resounding feet,
When wilt thou learn to feel?   O, what a brow
Were this to sparkle in some clime of laughter,
Where nothing wither'd, saving guilt and grief!
There it were lovely as the smile of seraphs
Descending heaven to bring a spirit home—
But here the paler the more beautiful—
This eye more wet with pity were more bright—
This voice more tremulous, most musical!

Mar. Sweet Annabelle, why dost thou weep ?
Ann.   Alas !
Has not each day borne weeds and widowhood
To every hamlet of romantic Seine?
Broke in the midst the lively vintage song,
And made it end in tears and lamentation ?
O, we have friends and brothers !
  Mar.   We have lost none.
  Ann.. We have the more to lose.   Those crimson
    streets
Of the dread city never will be dry
Till every eye and every throbbing vein
Has paid its tributary drop——Didst hear
That leaden sound come shuddering through the air ?
Didst hear it, Marguerite ?
  Mar.   Too true, I heard
The ceaseless voice of that inhuman engine
Telling its tale of death.
  Ann.   And canst thou guess
What spirit, newly freed, floats on the wind
That passes us ?   This morn we might have told
Each star that form'd the blessed constellation
About our hearts—How may we count them now ?
  Mar. Thy fancy is too busy.   More than this
I shar'd with thee at first, but frequent horrors
Have grown familiar ; and the worn in battle,
Though he can find a sigh for those who fall,
Forgets his fears for those *who may*.   E'en *thou*
Hast not been long a yellow leaf amidst

The purple wreath of mingling gaiety,
Circling our rustic homes. I've seen thee dash
Thy tears away, and seem the very soul
Of mirth and frolic innocence. E'en then
I've seen thee—when yon fatal sound, as now,
Brought its black mandate through the still, soft
        night,
To stay our steps, and cast an eye to heav'n—
Yield thy unclasped hand to him thou lov'st,
And force thyself to happiness again.
   Ann. True—I have much to mourn.
   Mar.   But yet not this—
Some recent grief reflects its vividness
Upon the fading colours of the past.
The time's gone by thou shouldst have been a bride :
And thou dost talk no more of the young soldier
Who was so dear a theme.
   Ann.   It is because
A worthless maiden's words cannot enrich him.
   Mar. Why art thou changed ?
   Ann.   I am too much the same.
   Mar. And he has proved unkind ?
   Ann.   O, not unkind !
Yet, if he were, what right have I to blame him ?
I had no claim upon his love—no more
Than the scorch'd pilgrim on the summer-breeze,
And could not chide it when it pass'd away,
Save with my tears.
   Mar.   And hath it pass'd away ?
Forget him, Annabelle.

Ann.   The wither'd flower
Forget the dew that bath'd its morning blossom—
The orphan'd heart forget its mother's breast!

Mar. Then will I lose thy love, and tell thee all.

Ann. Hold, I beseech thee, Marguerite, if aught
Thou'dst speak disparagingly of Eustache—
He never spoke so of his enemies.

Mar. But *does* so by his friends.   It is not just
To let thee mourn for what thou shouldst despise.
Thou dost remember the chateau hard by,
Whose airy pillars, from their spiry knoll,
Cleaved, as we fancied, the red streaky sun-set
Into square furnaces of flame?   We sat
Amidst the amphitheatre of vineyards,
Which, twining in their playful luxury,
Leap'd up to screen the low plebeian world
From its white walls and ruby-studded windows.
O, what soft words then mingled with thy soul,
Like breath of roses, with the breeze about us!
What joy and fondness danced in his dark eye,
As if they had been conjur'd into life
By the sweet music of responsive hearts!
I gazed apart upon the happiest pair
That ever sigh'd the twilight hour away.

Ann. Talk on—the memory of departed bliss
Is the most dear of sorrows.

Mar.   I employed
My solitude in watching your lips move,
And giving meaning to each gentle gesture.
I thought you playfully described some fair

And wealthier maid to his reluctant ear ;
Made her the mistress of that sweet chateau
And vineyard wilderness, then crown'd her worth
With love for him, *almost* as true as thine.

    Ann. I then could jest with him.

    Mar.   He look'd reproach,
Press'd your soft cheek to his, and fondly pointing
To yon small star which shone so constantly
Directly o'er your honeysuckled cottage,
Seem'd as he swore his happiness and fate
Were ruled by that and thee.

    Ann.   Well, Marguerite—
My tears prove how I listen.

    Mar.   I have done,
There *is* a mistress of that tempting home,
And the fair star that governs thy Eustache
Hath pass'd into another sphere.

    Ann.   And there
May it remain, and beauteous Mathilde
Prove worthy as most fortunate and lovely !

    Mar. Speak you so fondly of her ?

    Ann.   And why not ?
I loved her ere I did suspect the tale
Of which you deemed me ignorant ; and now
His love assures me that I judged her well.

    Mar. Sweet Annabelle, if she deserved your praise
She would not steal away your early hopes.
Could *you* be happy in the smiles of falsehood—
Receive the sighs of a cold, truant heart,
Whilst every one was wafting the faint life

From innocence that pined in virgin faith?
O, no! Be sure what he hath basely won
Will prove as base in value.

Ann.   Look—he comes!

Mar. He dares? Oh no, this cannot be Eustache!
How changed his spirit from the days of pride,
When conscious innocence upheld his head!
Falsehood and shame have crush'd him like a worm,
And riveted his once bold eye to the dust!

Ann. Leave me, I pray you—I would wish him
          happy,
Show I resent not—pardon him, and say
Farewell—much, much that shakes me to pronounce,
And him no jot to hear.   Nay, weep not for me,
It is an office I can do myself.
Young soul, and did I blame thee for not feeling?
Resume thy smiles, and never know the pang
To be forsaken?

ANNABELLE, EUSTACHE.

Ann.   Welcome, dear Eustache!
We have been strange of late.

Eus.   I have deserved
Reproach, and fear'd to meet it, Annabelle.

Ann. Reproach from *me!* O, never!

Eus.   Then you cease
To love?

Ann.   It is a useless question.   No,
I can be constant and ask no return.

Eus. I am a wretch whom you should scorn, not
    love,
And scarce have virtue to declare my vileness.
    Ann. Needs there excuse to me for choosing her
Whom you love best? Did I not always pray
That no devotion to a hasty promise
Should be as fatal to yourself as want
Of worth to me? Indeed, most dear Eustache,
I shall be happier to see you happy
With her you love, than wretched with myself.
    Eus. Thy shame for me hath spared my tongue
    what well
Might wither it. What shall I say, thou dear one?
(For dear thou art, though I am false to thee)
Entreat thee to forget? I who besought
Thy love so long—and bade thee swear, and told thee
What years of paradise each broken vow,
Like a loos'd fiend, drove withering from thy hopes!
And shall I urge thee to receive some other,
Who more deserves thee, to thy wounded bosom?
I who so often sigh'd upon that altar
My shadowy jealousy—my causeless dreams,
Of where thou *might'st* have lavish'd thy young love
Had we ne'er met? I who did fear to die
Lest I should leave my sacred place to one
Who might more dearly fill it?
    Ann.   O hush, hush!
Though I must love to hear of other times,
I would not buy the pleasure at thy pain.

O why shouldst *thou* look back ; who hast so much
Of joy before thee ?

  Eus.   Joy for me ?—in what ?
In constant fears that those in whom I trust
Will leave me to the loneliness of those
Who trusted *me* ? Is there a spot on earth,
A hue in heaven, which hath not something in it
Which we have dwelt upon together ? Something
To frown remembrance, penitence, despair ?
Is there a virtue blooming in this world
Which will not show thee in thy meek forgiveness ?
Is there a crime which will not make me shrink
By claiming kindred with the one 'gainst *thee* ?
Is there a beauty, bright above the rest,
Which will not tell me she whom I forsook
Possess'd it in a blush more paramount ?
O, Annabelle ! I came to thee in fear
But still prepared, and anxious for reproach :
Not to be cursed with pardon.

  Ann.   Must I not
Remain your friend ?—This morn, while yet the sun
Dwelt with a crimson mist upon our vineyard,
And purple clouds, like happy lovers, stole
With smiles and tears into each other's bosom,
I threw my lattice wide to drink the stream
Of liquid odours rolling from the south ;
And then came mix'd with it a marriage song,
Whose distant melody did seem to dance
Upon a hundred lips of revelry,

And bells and flageolets, and all the sounds
Befitting happiness and summer sunshine.
'Twas a strange thing to weep at, yet I wept—
I know not why.—Some weep for grief, and some
For joy—but I for neither, or for both
Mix'd in a feeling more beloved than either,
Which weigh'd my heart down like a drooping bough
O'erloaded with its luxury of roses.
And then— and then——the thoughts of silly maids
Run wilder than these roving vines—I found
My hands were clasp'd together, and my spirit
Stole from my eyes with a dim sense of prayer,
Which had no words.   I begg'd a gentle fortune
Upon the newly wedded—pray'd I not
For *thee*, Eustache ?

  Eus.   I thought I had no more
To tell thee.

  Ann.   Nor thou hast, Eustache ; I'll guess it.
I know not—I—I shall speak presently.
I pray thee think not that I grieve thou'rt happy ;
For e'en the victim that courts immolation
To win the garden, blooming with bright stars,
Will writhe beneath the blow that sends it thither.

  Eus. O, if thou meet'st the life that's due to thee,
How oft thou'lt drop a pitying tear for him
Who madly did desert his share of it !

  Ann. Not madly—no. Be cheerful, dear Eus-
    tache—
I shall do well enough—I must love still,
For that is life, and that thy bride will spare me ;

But here is that which I have worn for years,
Smiled with, and wept with, and almost believed
It understood me.   O, if 'twere but so,
And could but speak, I would enjoin it tell thee
Whene'er a truer heart did beat against it.
Take it—it is Mathilde's—but do not think
I yield it up in anger or in pride—
No, dear Eustache—no more than dwells within
The fond kiss given with it *then* and *now.*

    Eus. The first dear present of accepted love !
O, hide it—stamp on it—let it be dust—
For such I made the lineaments of one
More faithful, and, like thee, forsaken.

    Ann.   Ah !
The fierce Merzon ! Mathilde's deserted lover !
I have a chill foreboding—he hath ne'er
Enjoy'd the bliss of pardoning a wrong,
And has a heart that would not shrink from blood,
Though 'twere his father's.

    Eus.   He is freely welcome
To every drop of mine, for I do long
For some dire, speedy vengeance to o'ertake me.
Thou ne'er wilt know the shuddering of that pause
When guilt awaits its meed.

    Ann.   What men are these ?

    Eus. A troop of minions from the city bandits,
Reeking from carnage, and in search of fresh.

    Ann. O, wherefore should th' unhallow'd mis-
        creants
Bring here their death-denouncing steps ? Eustache,

Thou'st shown too oft thy manly indignation
Against the murderers—thou hast cross'd their path,
With speech and sword till thou hast roused their
       hate—
Ah me! thy virtue was enough for that!
Indeed thou must not meet them.

    Eus.   Nor avoid—
I scorn'd the wretches when my life was precious—
I have less need to fly them now.

    ANNABELLE, EUSTACHE, GERAULT, OFFICER,
           AND GENS-D'ARMES.

    Ger.   Eustache,
Thy hand—we once were comrades.
    Eus. (*turning from him*).   Once.
    Of.   Thou hast
Some certain friends, Eustache, who see with pity
Thy daily horror at these grievous times—
Some who would spare thee its continuance.

    Eus. 'Tis kind, indeed ; and, for the courtesy,
I'll pray for them and thee that you may find
The good you give, and that right speedily—
Come, sir, unfold.

    Ger.   Thou'rt summon'd to thy trial.
    Eus. Most rapid payment! fatal, but most just!
Sir, I am too straightforward to love forms—
Death cannot come more welcome than to him
That's out of love with life.   Your mock tribunal
Will never hear me plead to it, nor revel
In the sweet pastime of denying mercy

To suppliant Eustache ; therefore, at once,
Beseech you, feed your longing to behold
The blood that spurns you. (*To Annabelle*) Mute,
    thou faithful one!
Thou'lt not be so where tones like thine are heard.
On, sir—I am as ready to be led
As thou to lead me.
    Ger.   Now, by heaven, young soldier,
Thou'st made me hate my office. I have heard
The howling of a thousand recreants
Unmoved, but tamely to destroy the brave
Is the worst blot on bravery.
    Ann. (*rushing to him*).   Bless thee, bless thee !
Thou wilt return, and take, instead of blood,
All good men's prayers for ever !
    Ger.   Would I could——
But see (*pointing to his attendants*), 'tis past my
    power to befriend him ;
A word would make me partner in his fate.
    Ann. Art thou not human ?
    Of. (*advancing to Eustache*). We delay too long.
    Ann. (*flinging one arm round Eustache, and oppos-
    ing with the other*).
Stand off! who dares to place a villain's hand
Upon Eustache ? I can be proud as humble,
And will not sue to these for e'en thy life——
Do you not hear ? lead on !
    Eus.   And so farewell !
    Ann. Leave thee ! *I* leave thee ! Let Mathilde enjoy
Thy sunshine—in the storm thou'rt mine again !

Of. (*placing his hand upon her*). We must divide
    you.

Eus.   Hold! *(to Gerault).*   Thou 'rt less a
    wretch.
Lead her with kindness home, she 's young in sorrow,
And never learnt hard usage till I taught her.
Farewell, farewell!   [*Exit with the rest.*
  Ann. (*falling into the arms of Gerault*).
          Now thou art false indeed!

PART II.
Scene—*Montmartre.*
Annabelle, Gerault.

Ger. Rest—rest, poor maid.

Ann.   'Tis all one world of black,
No hill, no tower from its vapoury bed
Leaps up to mark the bounds of earth and heaven.
The stars too glide and glimmer underneath us
Like those above.   Where are we, gentle guide?

  Ger. Those lights are burning in the sleepless city.
This height thou 'st trod with happier feet ere now—
Bewilder'd girl, dost thou forget Montmartre?

  Ann. O, thou dost well remind me! for this scene
Is known as loved, and that is truly.   Here
Each summer eve I parted with Eustache,
And first did learn to weep.

  Ger.   And here, as then,
I 'd have thee think upon thy peaceful home,
And learn to smile again.

VOL. I.   F

Ann.   To smile! on whom ?
Thou madest a promise and an oath.   O think
How base is he who cheats the broken-hearted !
    Ger. Mistrust me not. I grieve, but will be faithful.
    Ann. So shalt thou gain a blessing which thou 'lt
        count
Amongst the sunbeams of a stormy life :
A scatter'd plank to save thee from despair
When seas of blood would overwhelm thy death-bed.
    Ger. Yet 'tis a fearful place thou 'dst have me show
        thee.
    Ann. And fearful is my need.   Thou'rt wavering
        still ;
Thine oath ! remember !
    Ger.   I suspect thy purpose
Is something desperate.   At thy feet, sweet maid,
I do beseech thy pity on thyself.
    Ann. Came I not here in pity of myself ?
Here lies our downward path.   I do believe
That thou wert made for tenderness and virtue,
And walk'd in crime by accident.   Alas !
I can but pay thy labour with my thanks.

A Prison.
EUSTACHE AND GUARD.

    Eus. The hours pass slowly—tell me, if you will,
How near my last approaches ?
    Guard.   It is midnight
Already.
    Eus.   The last minute that was granted

To my desire, and yet Mathilde not here?
I did entreat a swifter messenger.

    Guard. Perhaps the maid is wise, and better loves
To meet new friends than say farewell to old.

    Eus. And wilt thou jeer the dying? If thy soul
Were not too crusted in with blood and murder
I could relate enough to make it human.

    Guard. So every one of you believes his fate
The hardest; and, for partings and last wills,
And whatsoe'er comes readiest, implores
Fresh work for the tribunal's ministers,
To wait and watch till he hath heart to die.

    Eus. Was it for dread of death I ask'd to live?
Thou slanderer! What if the same wild day
Beheld thee wreathed in blushing bridal fetters,
Then saw them sudden changed to links of iron,
And these so soon to yield their victim up
To bondage in a blood-bedappled shroud?
Wouldst thou not long for some fond faithful ear,
To listen while thou saidst, "These things are strange?"

    Guard. But still this wonderer comes not.

    Eus.   Poor Mathilde!
Wedded and widow'd in a day, thy spirit
Hath too much woman in it not to sink;
Thou canst not come. Yet she whom I forsook
Was firm and fond enough to share my dungeon!
—I heard a knocking!

    Guard.   'Twas the workman's hammer
Joining the sledge that bears thee to thy doom:
Thou art more honour'd than the herd of culprits.

Eus. (*in deep thought*). I tempted thee to false-
      hood—Can it be
Thou wert too apt a pupil? Fie! 'tis savage
To doubt thy truth ere yet the virgin blush
Hath left thy cheek. Thou wilt be here.—A cry!—
   Guard. It is the rabble crowding round the portal
To see thee pass. The guard is turning out.
   Eus. My heart beats strangely lest she should not
      come!
   Guard. Why, thou dost shake!
   Eus.   No matter, say 'tis fear;
And though thou liest I will not tell thee so—
My mind's too busy to care what thou think'st—
                       [*relapsing.*
I cannot die till I have heard thee swear
Eternal hatred of the foe whose hand
In secret malice writes me down for carnage;
I cannot die till I have bade thee love
The poor—poor injured Annabelle (*knocking*). Thou
      heard'st?
It is a knocking, and now death is over—
And I'm in heaven. My wife! Mathilde!
           [*The door opens, and Merzon enters.*
                       Merzon!
   Mer. Thou sent'st a message to Mathilde, Eustache.
   Eus. And did she fix on thee to bring the answer?
   Mer. Did she not well to choose so dear a friend?
I have been comforting the wedded maid,
And come to say how well she is resign'd
To give thee to a better world.

Eus.   *Thou* comfort her ?
The loathed, the spurn'd Merzon, whom, Heave
    judge me,
I pitied for the distance I did fling him !

   Mer. Thou wert indeed *almost* victorious ;
Therefore 'twas needful to remove thee quickly.

    Eus. And wilt thou boast thou wert not brave
    enough
To meet me with an equal manliness ?

   Mer. Were the wrong equal, so were our conten-
    tion ;
We do not yield the robber stab for stab.
List, for thy time is brief.   Thou didst believe
That thou wert wed to never-dying faith,
Which, shadow-like, would follow all thy fortunes
With equal steps—presumptuous aspirant !
What claim had'st thou to excellence so far
Above the reach of more deserving men ?
Thy truth to her to whom thou first wert plighted ?
What hope ? thy bride's tried constancy to *me* ?
Alas ! thou 'lt find her weak and wavering
As thou thyself.

    Eus.   Thou shameless and despised !
If such the prize, why has the loss of it
Thus driven thee to damn thyself ?

    Mer.   'Twas said
I lov'd the maid—'twas true—I lov'd her beauty.
'Twas said she had discarded me for thee ;
And this was true. Now tell when mortal man
Hath laid his hand on aught that pleas'd the will

Or deck'd the honour of Merzon, and lived ?
What more ?   I pass'd into the revel throng,
And sate me by the mistress of the feast.
Some marvell'd that thy absence should so far
Belie thy promise, some that thy place was fill'd
By *me*, the whilst the bride spoke tremblingly
To bid me welcome to the wedding cheer.

    Eus. To make thee scorned of others as of her.

    Mer. The time went by—the pausing mirth re-
        vived,
And all believed I came in friendliness
To banish idle fears of my revenge ;
While, 'midst the busy sounds of lute and song,
I told my grief, and woke a soft remorse
In her who listened.

    Eus.   And who listen'd only
For a defender from thy cursed tongue.

    Mer. She sigh'd and wept—" She knew not half
        my love,
She had been rash ; yet, since the deed was done,
We must henceforth meet only in our prayers."
At length comes one with ghastly face to tell
The dire mischance which had befall'n the bridegroom ;
And there were wonder and becoming woe,
And tears in some, and prophecies recalled,
Which beldames muttered ere you left the altar —
How two false-hearted never could be blest,
And sudden wrath would follow.   And what then ?
The scared Mathilde sobb'd loudly with affright
And disappointment of her marriage hopes ;

Whilst I renew'd the offer of my love,
And kind forgetfulness of all the past.
   Eus. Ay, and she spurn'd thee.
   Mer.   No ; she was too thankful.
   Eus. O, my good guard, be blest, and loose my
      chains
One instant whilst I tear this liar piecemeal.
   Mer. Alas, poor youth, thou hast not strength
      enough
To carry thine own weight ! I will have done.
A season pass'd in pitiful remembrance,
And decent weeds, shall faithfully be paid thee ;
Nor will I chide her if, in after times,
She drops a wandering tear upon thy tomb,
Or lulls me with the strain you taught her.
   Eus.   Monster
He hath destroy'd her, or she had been here
To scare him back to hell !
   Mer.   She *is* come here
To witness what I speak.   Behold the ring
Which made you one.   She drew it from her finger
With horror, lest some unimagined judgment
Should fall upon the wearer ; and returns it
By me, with pray'rs, that thou wilt die repentant.
        (*To himself, as he walks slowly out, looking
           steadily back upon Eustache*).
Ay ! doth he writhe ?——he made me *live* in torment ;
And thus in torment will I have *him die.*
   Eus. (*Clasping his hands*). Be merciful, and teach
     me, ere I die,

That this bad man doth wrong her!

Guard.   Come, prepare.

Eus. Not yet—not yet.

Guard.   We have delay'd too long.

I do endanger my own safety.

Eus.   Oh!

If thou dost die for sparing me one hour,

Thy sins will be forgiven!

Guard.   Impossible—

I pity thee, but have no power to spare.

Eus. (*kneeling*). Look—look—I kneel to thee, and
        thou dost weep.

I am afraid to die.

Guard.   Thou hast been brave;

Go nobly to thy death.

Eus.   And so I will,

Let me but know my wife is innocent,

My blood shall gush with laughter from my veins!

        EUSTACHE, GUARD, GENS-D'ARME.

Eus. Now, now, my messenger, let loose thy
        words,

Like one that's pleading for his life.   Thou saw'st
Mathilde.

Gens d'Arme. And did thy message—

Eus.   And the answer?

Gens d'Arme. The lady wept, and said a friend
        would bring it.

      (*Eustace dashes himself upon the ground*).

I've seen Eustache stand boldly in the battle.

Guard. Would he had died there! it hath wrung
    my heart
To look upon his anguish.   His accuser
Was here but now to crush him with the news
Of his young bride's unworthiness.   I would
Have stabb'd the wretch; but dar'd not for his
    power.
    Gens d'Arme. His case is hard—'twere best to free
    him quickly.
Come, rouse him.
    Guard.   Now for pity do't thyself;
I'm only fit for common cruelties.
    Gens d'Arme. Why, man, he hath a comrade in his
    death
Would move thee more—a delicate young boy,
And lovely as a maiden.   I look'd on
The whilst he stood before our dread tribunal;
And when maturer victims groan'd and wept,
His cheek seem'd pale with sorrow more than fear:
He heard his sentence with a smile, and ask'd
No mercy saving leave to empt his veins
In the same current with Eustache.   He comes,
I could not harm a thing so beautiful.
    Guard. Who hath denounced him?
    Gens d'Arme.   None that I could hear;
I saw him pressing through the crowd to join
A string of criminals who stood for sentence,
And there, in spite of one who strove to hold him
With tears and prayers, he gain'd what seem'd his
    wish.

                            F 5

THE ABOVE.   ANNABELLE (*as a peasant boy*),
  GERAULT, GUARDS, &c.

Ann. (*Rushing to Eustache, bends over him, and*
        speaks in a suppressed tone).
Thou 'rt mine at last—our blood will now be wedded
In a sweet stream, sacred to faithful love !
                              [*The death-bell tolls.*
  Eus. (*Springing up.*) Mathilde, Mathilde ! are
        there so many here,
And thou away ?
  Ger.   Be patient, good Eustache ;
If she forgets thee, thou art still béloved
As never man hath been.
  Eus.   I hear thee not !
I cannot for the beating of my heart ;
He said he was to marry her ! my wife !
O, no, no, no ! which of you all will gain
The blessing of a dying man, and say
That she is dead ?
  [*He sinks overpowered upon the bosom of Annabelle.*
  Ann.   He hath forgotten *me.*
  Eus. Why do we stay ? on, on, sweet friends, to
        death,
For I am braver than the reeking Mars,
And scent my own blood with a raven's longing !
Pale, faithful, and forsaken Annabelle,
Was it for this I blanch'd thy blooming cheek ?
Come hither one of you—I have a word
Of special trust (*to Annabelle*).   There is a gentle girl
Who hath been faithful to me since the day

When first her eye look'd love and loveliness.
Succeeding years bestow'd their tribute graces,
And with each grace, it seem'd, increasing fondness;
Till radiant womanhood had made her perfect.
Well then, I snatch'd the prize, and with a soul
Tumultuous in its passionate gratitude
Fell down and shudder'd my wild thanks to Heaven?
Fool, fool and villain! She was *won*—what more
Could such an idiot wish for? I forsook her,
Forgot at once her tenderness and tears,
And married with another. O, good youth,
Teach me some dying message to this maid
Of fitting sorrow and reviving love;
For I am bow'd with humbleness, and have
No power to instruct thee.
    Ann.   Shall I say
Thou hast resumed thy faith?
    Eus.   She will not trust thee.
Say, if thou canst, whate'er a dying man
Can feel when those he cherish'd have proved false,
Those he deserted true.
    Ann.   Thy Annabelle
Believes and is most blest! now we will go
In triumph to our bridal's crimson altar,
And with commingling spirits gaze upon
Our nuptial moon in Paradise.
    Ger.   'Tis true;
This faithful maid is come to die with thee.
    Eus. Hold, let me breathe—my Annabelle? to
        die?
To die with me? O, pity me, ye heavens!

Ann. It is in vain; thou canst not leave me now.
Yon grave tribunal, gentler than Eustache,
Did hear my prayers, and framed a crime for me
Which I confess'd, more gladly than my love
When first you ask'd it — (*to Gerault*).   Take my
　　　　latest thanks.
At morn seek out the youthful Marguerite,
And tell my story, with this fond addition:
I left no dearer friend than her and thee.
Thy hand, most dear Eustache.
　　Eus.　　　　　　Ye vengeful powers,
Requite my guilt less terribly! 'Tis just
I suffer, but is death too little? Must I
Know the last eye that would have wept my fall
Closes untimely with my own? The voice—
The only voice that had excused thy wrongs,
And smoothed my name, can utter no lament?
O, mercy, mercy! let not one so soft
Inflict a pang so deadly.
　　Ann.　　　　　　Thou 'lt forgive me.
My heart betray'd, or I had died with thee
An unknown partner.
　　Eus.　　　　　Mercy! yet, no mercy!
O, that white brow, and those sweet raven braids,
Which have reposed upon my heart so oft—
A moment hence, and where will they repose?
Where, where that delicate, devoted form
Which the vile mob shall stand to gaze upon,
And wonder what the features might have been?
'Tis the last time that mortal lips shall touch them.
　　　　　　　　　[*Clasping her violently.*

Ann. (*The death-bell tolling*). Hark to that sound !
    it is our marriage peal !

Eus. Sweet Annabelle !

Ann.   Come, come, the choir is waiting
To sing us into paradise !

Eus.   O, God !

  [*They go out hand in hand, followed by the rest.*

WILD WATER POND.

There is a magnet-like attraction in
These waters to the imaginative power,
That links the viewless with the visible,
And pictures things unseen.
Campbell.

In the early part of my life, I was fond of
sporting, and possessed an adventurous turn of
mind, which frequently led me many days'
journey from home, exploring the country,
with little care for any means of subsistence
beyond my dogs and gun. In one of these
rambles, about the month of December, I continued to follow my game far into the Low
Counties, where I was swamped and bewildered amongst wild fowl of every description.
My eagerness led me on and on, I knew not
whither, till I found myself, towards dusk, in

the middle of a large moor, which seemed destined to be my bed for the night. The prospect was not very comfortable, for I was wet through, and well nigh starved.

Whilst musing what was to become of me, I reached the broken towing path of an old, and apparently deserted, river, for I could perceive no recent trace of horses, and a dilapidated lock, hard by, was covered with moss, as though it had not been opened for a month. I took my seat upon the decayed handle of the gate, and looked wistfully along the banks, in the faint hope of spying some solitary barge which might supply my necessities. Fortune was disposed to favour me ; for, as my eye gradually rose towards the cold, blue distance, I could distinctly see a little column of moving smoke. In a moment afterwards, I discovered a red night-cap, and heard the smack of a whip. Never did any thing come more opportunely.

In a few minutes the boat arrived at the lock. It was laden with coals, but my habits had rendered me not over difficult as to accommodation, and it answered my purpose as well as could be wished. The captain, who was likewise all the attendants, excepting a ragged boy who flogged the horses, was an intelligent fellow enough for his kind, and informed me that I was ten or a dozen miles from the nearest house, which it was impossible for me to find, and twenty from Wild Water Pond, whither he was bound. As he described the country onwards to be a grand rendezvous for wild ducks, and it signified very little in which direction I travelled, I stepped on board, and took up my quarters in his little smoky cabin.

My companion had been chosen for his present occupation (for which beings of civilized regions would have had little fancy) from the vagrant tribes of those parts, who were in the habit of being driven about from place to place by the floods, and my predilections for wandering appeared to win much upon his regard. He told me long stories of the weariness of working a barge along a river where nothing was moving, and how it was only supportable in winter time, when it was cold sleeping under a hedge, and the fowls went home to roost, and suppers were scarce. He consoled himself likewise with the reflection that it was excellent sport to steal after the wild birds, occasionally with an old brass fire-lock, six feet long, and stocked up to the muzzle, and that, if the place was lonely, there was the less danger of interruption from gamekeepers and justices of the peace. Things, however, were shortly to undergo a vast revolution. All the bog which I saw to the right and left was to be turned into parks and pleasure-grounds, all the peat holes were to be fish ponds, and every bulrush was to spring up into an oak tree. And then for fine houses! they were to stand as thick as daisies! Upon inquiring who was to perform all these prodigies, I was told that they were to be the work of the great man who had built a house in the Pond.

This great man, it appeared, was not very great yet, but meant to be so shortly. He had the character of having undertaken wonderful projects which no one else had ever thought of, and, though they had never yet repaid his pains, he was allowed on all hands to be the greatest genius in the world, and sure to be strangely rich some day or other. In other words, he had been an unsuccessful speculator, and was determined to persevere until he made or marred himself.   Amongst other wise calculations, he had taken it into his head that it was cheaper to buy water than land, and had purchased Wild Water Pond, an interminable sheet of that element, only broken by a few beds of bulrushes, and small islands of quagmire, for the purpose of draining it, and planting it, and doing heaven-knows-what with it, till both the lord and the land were to thrive for all the world like Jack and the bean stalk.

Like speculators in general, Mr. Carrol, which was the wise man's name, was too much occupied to consider the comforts of those who depended upon him, and had brought a patient, gentle-hearted wife, to recruit a sickly constitution in the strong holds of typhus and the ague.   There was likewise a young lady whom he called his daughter, but who went by another name.   From this I concluded that the mother had been married twice, and had probably herself been the subject of a speculation, and made her fortune a stepping-stone to the Pond, in which they stood so good a chance of sinking together. All this gave me but sorry prepossessions of Mr. Carrol, and I could learn nothing better, excepting that he did good by employing the poor upon his embankments, and setting the boats to work to bring necessaries which could come by no other means. Our cargo of coals was intended to keep the rot out of these identical walls; and, when it was delivered, I could either return by the same conveyance, or remain at the Wild Water Lock House and take a lesson in making a fortune.

Our voyage continued through the night, and, at daybreak, the aspect of the country, as far as I could judge through the dense vapours, had only changed for the worse, the bog extending from about ten feet below the bed of the river even up to the horizon. The increased myriads of water-fowl showed that every step we advanced was farther and farther from the haunt of human beings. By degrees, the green, oozy sod became more intersected by stagnant pools, which continued to grow wider, till the whole country opened upon us like a boundless ocean. About it, as I have before said, were various clusters of wild, willowy islands, and on one of these, which was of the most considerable extent, arose the forlorn white walls of a newly-built mansion. As I gazed upon the desolate abode, I could not restrain an expression of indignation at the heartless being who could hope to prosper by this abandonment of all domestic solicitude. Had he come here by himself, I could have pardoned and pitied him for a madman; but to bring others, who showed, by their compliance, that they were worthy of better fates, was an offence for which, my companion agreed with me, he ought to have had his house tied about his neck and been smothered in his own swamp.

The Lock House, at which I was to lodge, was a small, ruinous hut, inhabited by an old couple, who were sore stricken with the rheumatism, and received me upon crutches. The sight of a human face seemed to rejoice their hearts, for they told me that, though their prospect would be mighty fine in summer, if it were not for the gnats, people had no great admiration for the country thereabouts. As for the great man, nobody came to see him. All the world were afraid of him, because he was so wonderfully clever and had dug such deep ditches.

Good souls! They had stuck to their home as tenaciously as a brace of dab chicks, and had never left it except to bury their children, who had all been subject to sore throats. They loved to dabble about their old nest. They had employment in keeping the keys of the Lock, and doctoring their rheumatisms. They had amusement in setting eel pots in the waste water, which tumbled through their pen into the great man's Pond (a circumstance which added materially to his draining avocations); and they had the satisfaction of having grown lusty, which showed that, barring the aforesaid rheumatism, the place agreed with their constitutions. No wonder, then, that these contented and untravelled persons were somewhat astonished by the genius of such a magician as Mr. Carrol, who had astonished all the wild geese and water rats in the country. Before I had been half an hour domesticated, I had heard wonders enough to petrify me, and my interest for this strange person's family, which was considerably heightened by the description of the daughter, increased into a determination of knowing something about them. Having, therefore, expressed my obligations to my friend of the barge, and acquainted him that it was not my intention to return with him, I committed myself to a crazy mud boat, and pushed off to shoot, and meditate how to scrape acquaintance.

In my progress I saw hosts of half naked wretches, toiling up to their eyes in slime and slough ; but I could not perceive that the water-mark had sunk one jot from its original height, and Mr. Carrol's bargain seemed by no means to improve upon acquaintance. The only crop which it was ever likely to yield was of ducks and geese, of which, indeed, there was an abundance, which very soon put the proprietor and his concerns quite out of my head. I followed them from island to island, sometimes punting and sometimes wading, according to the depth of the water, which varied constantly from six inches to twice the number of feet, till, as usual, I found myself benighted,

Fortunately, the great man's house was not shut up, and, while this was the case, there was no possibility of losing sight of his lights, for which I straightway directed my course. It was no bad opportunity for gratifying my curiosity by introducing myself as a benighted traveller, and I moored my shallop within a few yards of the window. The room was large, and barely furnished, and, like the handiwork of speculators in general, unfinished. Mr. Carrol was sitting at the table. He was a square built, middle-aged, man, dressed in a short green jacket and high mud boots. His countenance was dark, forbidding, and disappointed; and his manner, when he muttered a few words over a plan or calculation, which was lying before him, seemed abrupt and petulant. His wife sat opposite to him with her work, and formed a strong contrast. She was handsome and mild looking, like one whose fate was ordained to be ruled by others, and the pale melancholy of her cheek bore witness that this rule had not always been in unison with her inclinations. By the fire, with her hands before her, as though her thoughts were too busy to allow them occupation, and her eyes turning from one to the other of her companions, with alternate fondness and indignation, sat the daughter. Her features were handsome like her mother's, but there was a decision of character about them which rendered them far more remarkable, particularly in one so young. Her fine dark eye was full of impetuous feeling, and her whole person was of the stamp which nature is wont to place upon spirits of unusual order. This was a being worth knowing ; and, in despite of a blunderbuss and several other weapons which were hanging over the fire-place, I rang boldly at the door.

The house was so formed that I could see into the room even here. The party looked at each other in considerable surprise at the prospect of a visiter, and well they might, for, to say nothing of the scanty neighbourhood, the approach to their abode was calculated to make people call at seasonable hours, if it produced no other advantage. Before the door was opened, I saw Carrol move closer to his depôt of arms, where he stood frowning and listening to the parley between me and the servant. As I told my tale of distress he evidently uttered an exclamation of impatience, and his wife as evidently besought him to invite the stranger to his fireside. The younger lady said nothing, save what was conveyed in a look of contempt at the inhospitality of her step-father. Finally, Mr. Carrol came to the door himself, and, with a scowling sort of courtesy, desired me to walk in till he procured a guide for me.

The story of my appearance in those regions was a necessary fill-up of the interval before the guide and lantern were ready, and I soon contrived to dissipate all suspicions of evil designs. The speculator talked a few disjointed words about dark nights and deep waters, made a few unintelligible allusions to the arts of draining and planting, and, by degrees, dropped off to his plan. The conversation went on well enough without him, while the only indication of his knowing what it was about was an occasional deep-mouthed fragment, and sometimes merely a scowl. It was clear enough that he hated company and con-

versation, which disturbed his calculations;
but the gentleness of his wife, and the brilliant spirit of her daughter, made his ab-
straction a matter of small import. I was welcomed by the former as an acceptable addition
to their neighbourhood, and the latter completed her mother's meaning, with an assurance
that their situation could hardly be called retired, when they were within five miles of a
village, which the floods permitted them to
approach at least three or four times in the
year. To be sure, they had not always taken
advantage of these opportunities, because Mr.
Carrol was sometimes unable to spare a boat
from his workmen to convey them to the towing path; but then the old people from the
Lock House came once a month to be cured
of the ague, and altogether their situation was
very charming.

There was a sweetness of voice and fondness
of manner towards her mother, which contrasted strangely in this beautiful girl with the
fearless sarcasm which she now and then
levelled at Carrol, and I was almost in doubt
whether she was most to be admired or dreaded.

I longed to have opportunities for judging, and endeavoured to bespeak favour and future invitations by entering into the projector's plans. I declared (Heaven forgive me!) that they were, somehow or other, likely to be of great benefit to mankind; and Carrol, though a great speculator, being no considerable genius, suffered me very easily to entrap him into a permission to inspect the dykes and drains by which his name was to swim down to posterity. I took my leave with numerous acknowledgments, and was made happy by a growl and a nod, which I considered a little more friendly than my reception had been.

Long after I had retired to bed, the images of Carrol and his wife, with the striking beauty and vivacity of her daughter, kept flitting through my mind in a kind of waking dreaminess, which was any thing but rest. The first was evidently a low-born man, of a coarse, unfeeling, character; tyrannical to those who would permit him to be so, and very easily to be cowed by those who withstood him. This was clearly made out in his opposite manner to the two latter, upon whose uncomfortable

G 2

prospects I continued to dwell till I almost
wished that I had not introduced myself, and
then to devise impossible, knight-errant plans
for their deliverance.

I rose early in the morning, and, having
equipped myself as decently as my wardrobe
permitted, wandered restlessly up and down
the river till it was time to take advantage of
Carrol's courtesy; that is to say, till I had
watched him out to the superintendence of his
workmen.   I then darted my punt over to the
Mansion of the Moss, and was shown in to the
objects of my somewhat hasty concern.

I was received, I thought, with more pleasure
and less restraint than such a stranger might
have expected. Had it been more in the world,
I should probably not have had so much to
boast of; but, in a desert, the sight of a human
face, however unworthy, is no insignificant
event.   I soon found myself perfectly acquainted, and lost no time in adding a thousand rivets
to the fetters which had been cast over me at
first sight.   The spirit of Lucy, which had appalled me the night before, was, in the absence
of her step-father, subdued to all the gentle-

ness of her mother. The talent which was burning in her large hazel eyes seemed rather to court concealment than display; the modest diffidence with which she uttered her opinions was beautiful as the blush upon her cheek; and the nature of her whole manner showed, that her disposition was equally proof against the gift of transcendent loveliness. She was the very opposite of what I had been led to expect—she was far more than I had yet power to conceive. Her feelings were no less various than her personal attractions, and her devotion to those whom she loved was only to be matched by her disregard for every thing which appertained to herself. Solitude, so uncongenial to a young and affectionate heart, nay, even oppression, she could have borne with resignation; but when these evils were applied to her uncomplaining mother— when she saw her spirit broken, her health declining, her meek and sorrowful retrospections to the comfort which she had sacrificed, with her quiet endeavours to make the most of the little which was left—her blood leaped up against the unfeeling cause of it all, and her tongue was armed with bitterness proportionate to his incapacity to appreciate it. These, in their full extent, were after observations; but, on the morning of which I am speaking, they were shadowed out sufficiently to convince me that Lucy was the purest embodiment of feeling which I had yet beheld. Her mind was a cloudless sky, and every thought a star.

My visit was long, and only interrupted by Carrol towards its conclusion. He came in with no very prepossessing countenance, confounding the rain which was filling his pond as fast as he baled it out, and vowing stoutly that he would go to law with the proprietors of the river for giving him the benefit of their waste water. After he had expended somewhat of his choler, or rather restrained it under the influence of Lucy's keen glance of irony, he turned to me with a nod of recognition, and entered into his usual style of conversation, breaking every half sentence with a reference to his pocket book, as if he were all the time reckoning how many pails full were yet to be thrown out of his everlasting pond. He gave me to understand, as far as I could gather, that

he was not sorry to see me, nor yet particularly glad——that I might do well enough to talk
to the ladies, to whom he had no time to talk
himself, and that I might suit my convenience
either in coming or staying away. I was not
to mind him, because he should not mind me,
which would make things pleasant for all parties,
and, perhaps, prevent his hearing any more
complaints as to want of society.

The Lock House then was to be my home for
a longer period than I had expected. When I
returned to it, I found my good genius of the
coal-boat preparing for another cruise through
the bogs, and I took advantage of the opportunity to supply myself with the various con-
veniences of which I stood in need.

My visits to the Mansion of the Moss were
constant, and our acquaintance became more
and more familiar, till the omission of a day
was a subject of playful remonstrance. Even
Carrol, though he kept his word, and took little
more notice of me than he would have done of
a lap-dog, appeared to grow more friendly, now
and then sported a rough joke, and once or
twice, when the weather was fine, and the

sinking of his pond had caused a corresponding rise in his spirits, invited me to dine with him, and discuss the progress of his improvements. On these occasions I saw more of the man's character than I should perhaps have discovered under other circumstances. He drank freely, and would then lose sight of his habitual caution, and shake off his taciturnity. This, however, by no means improved my opinion of him, for the more his mind opened, the more dark and repulsive it appeared. His choice themes of conversation, next to his dykes, and the lawsuit which he had commenced against the waste water, were the abuse of his two innocent victims, the one of whom he affected to despise for imbecility, while he hated the other for repaying that contempt upon himself. He did not wish to conceal that he had married for money to carry on his speculations, and detailed, with a brutal exultation, the means by which he had won his unsuspecting wife, and how she had begun to repent her bargain too late. He would then work himself up into anger, and demand whether it was not a hard case that some of her money was still beyond his power, and intended for her termagant daughter; and finally wish that the ague or the typhus fever would fly away with them both together. Many a time did I burn to dash the bottle down the ruffian's throat, but my admission to the house depended upon my keeping terms with him, and I used to listen patiently till he was well sotted and had dropped off to sleep.

Contrary to all our expectations, the waste water cause was decided in his favour, and he really showed, for a day or two, something like a happy face. His exultation, when he marshalled his workmen to dam up the sluice, was beyond all bounds, and he was confident that, by that day-month, there would not be a drop of water in *his park*. In less than a week, a bank was raised as impenetrable as the walls of Tyre, and there was not a person present who surveyed it without perfect admiration—except, indeed, my old friends of the Lock House, who assured me, with much lamentation, that their fishing was entirely spoiled.

After the embankment was finished, I returned with Carrol to dinner. He did the

honours of his house so well, that I could almost fancy how his wife came to be deceived
into marrying him, and his victims gazed upon
him, as much as to say, "Why can you not
always be thus?" The only drawback upon
our pleasure was a heavy shower of rain, which
continued all the evening to patter against the
window, as though it threatened to avenge the
cause of the river.

"Ay, ay!" exclaimed Carrol, every five
minutes, "I hear you! How that cursed sluice
would be pouring now if its mouth were not
stopped!"

When I left them for the night, the rain was
coming down in a deluge, and the wind beat
me about fearfully. I could scarcely accom-
plish the voyage to my cabin, and when I
arrived there I was half drowned. It was as
wild a storm as I had ever witnessed; and,
when I lay down in my bed, I had serious
doubts whether our little building was not
going to take flight. Nevertheless, I dropped
off asleep.

I believe my slumbers continued to bid defiance to the elements till two or three o'clock.

About this time, I was awakened by the most tremendous uproar I ever heard. At first, I could not make out what it was. I started up, and shouted to my old landlord, but both he and his partner had already hopped out upon their crutches to see whether the world was over, and I threw on my clothes as hastily as I could to follow their example.

The storm had ceased, and the bright moon-shine settled our doubts, as to what was the matter, at the first glance. The happy result of Carrol's lawsuit, and his excellent dam, had been the accumulation of more water than the river could hold. About a hundred yards of the old rotten bank had given way at a crash; and now, as my host of the Lock very sensibly observed, instead of having a pretty little fall of waste water, which would have purled beautifully through his park, whenever it might have merited such a title, he had got the whole river, all at once, and, for the future, was about as likely to drain it off as he was to drink it. The sight and the sound were really awful. The old river bellowed like a wounded giant, and the tide of life leaped from his side in a foaming cataract, which bade fair to spoil him of his last drop. The whole morass was a sheet of living wrath, in which the struggling osier beds lay down supinely, whilst the wild birds wheeled about in greater astonishment than ever. In the midst of the turmoil, I heard the vociferations of the conjurer who had brought this wonder to pass, and presently I saw him making his way to the scene of action in a punt, which ever and anon spun round like a tee-totum in the petty whirlpools, and obliged him to seek relief in oaths which might have appalled the river itself.

It was not long before the whole ragged population of the bogs came hovering about us in dismay, like ghosts which had been sore pressed by an inundation of the Styx. Carrol rushed to and fro despairingly, exhorting them to set to work and perform impossibilities. The breach could not have been filled up in a month ; and, indeed, such an operation, if it could have been performed in a moment, was now too late. The mischief was done, and nothing remained but to stand still and admire it. In this situation of things, the morning broke upon us, brilliant and sunny, as if on purpose to show the promising state of the park, of which but one small spot was visible, and that was the one whereon the house stood. All other objects were merely indicated by the bustle which they made under the water, which displayed nothing but eddies of white foam.

Carrol ground his teeth and bent his brow at this complete survey, in grim silence, as though he could not invent curses bitter enough to express his feelings. The first words which he uttered were execrations against his wife, for having given him money to gain his lawsuit—then against the water, for not rising, whilst it was in the mood, above his chimney top, and drowning all his plagues together, that he might begin the world afresh—then against all the nations in the globe, for not having furnished a precedent to guard him against such an un-looked-for catastrophe—and, finally, against himself, for not having been satisfied when he was well off, and unshackled by lands, wives, or daughters. As soon as he had uttered this sweeping malediction, and puzzled his busy myrmidons with a thousand absurd and oppo-

site directions, he observed that his last spot
of earth was growing less and less, and hastened homeward to scowl his household Gods
into a panic.

When he arrived, the enraged speculator was
doomed to find things worse and worse. The
land-springs in his cellars had burst, and inun-
dated all the lower part of the house, knee-
deep. The waters were still rising, and Mrs.
Carrol and Lucy were hiding themselves in the
bed-rooms, in momentary expectation of being
swept away. In spite of her terrors, the latter
could not restrain a smile of irony and sup-
pressed merriment, when orders were issued
for packing up for flight, the increased urgency
for which fulfilled her most sanguine wishes.
Carrol's mortal enemy, the old river, was remorselessly pursuing him from stair to stair, as
he staggered up to deposit his goods and chattels
in the garrets, and the chairs and tables were
beginning to float topsy-turvy out of the drawing-room window. The preparations, as may be
supposed, were not long in arrangement; and
a punt was brought in at the hall door to the
foot of the stairs. When I had handed the

ladies in, and was going to push off, I called out to Carrol, to apprise him that every thing was ready.

"Then go along with them," he shouted, from a distant part of the house.

"But whither are we to go?" I inquired.

"To the devil, if you like!" responded the ruffian; and we left him to manage his affairs as he might. As we quitted the devoted walls, the stream was whirling up to their base; and our motion gave them the appearance of having already set sail. Carrol, at the same time, thrust his head from a garret-window, to present a telescope at his cataract, which was running as merrily as ever; and, awful as matters were, there was still something in this great man's washing himself out of house and home, which was mightily ridiculous. Even the melancholy Mrs. Carrol could scarcely help being amused.

As we proceeded towards the dry land, we held a consultation as to what was to become of us; and, indeed, it was something of a mystery—for it was out of the question to suppose that the miserable assemblage of hovels, called the village, could afford accommodation. In this dilemma, we were obliged to call in my travelled friend of the coal-boat, who, as usual, was at no loss. In the course of his summer wanderings, he had pitched his tent on a choice spot of earth, called The Dark Common, from the umbrageous patches of wild oaks, and the ancient furze, which matted over the green roads in endless luxuriance. It was now in all its scented beauty of young leaves and yellow blossoms; and, on a gentle slope, which expanded its bosom to the soft south, stood a small fairy-formed villa, half hidden in the flowers which stole lovingly up its trelliced veranda, and echoing with the concert of a thousand guardian nightingales.

This pretty gem, it appeared, the last time that our friend had inspected the hen-roost, was not inhabited, and the chances were that it was vacant still. Lucy was charmed with the description. The sight of a tree, and the song of a bird, were blessings which she had never expected to enjoy again; and we commenced our voyage down the river with a prospect of reaching our destination in good time.

The sun shone out brightly ; and, after a few miles, the country began to promise better things. The river gradually sank into a level with green meadows, parted from each other by little obstreperous brooks, and sprinkled with cattle. Here and there a white-blossomed thorn gave token of more mature cultivation ; and presently the young elms were seen out-growing their dwarf neighbours of the hedge-row, and breaking the blue horizon with the swelling outlines and tender tints of spring. The scene of freshness and life was truly heart-cheering to me, after the dreary regions in which I had passed the winter ; but in Mrs. Carrol and Lucy, who had been doomed to them for three years, the effect which it created was inexpressible. The hurried and troubled con-versation with which we had set out had sunk to repose, like the clouds above us, and the feelings which had impelled it had melted into an exquisite calm. The silence was only broken by the unwonted notes of the lark and the cuckoo ; and, as we stole through the soft labyrinths of increasing flower and foliage, the warm blood trembled in Lucy's cheek, and her bright eyes declined as though she could have wept. I gazed upon her listless and unconscious beauty, without daring to breathe a word, lest I should break a thread of the en‑ chanting spell which it had cast over me. I loved to dwell upon it, without the intrusion of other thoughts—to expand my whole soul to its influence—for, in proportion as I discovered my ability to value Lucy, I valued myself.

In this happy mood we continued our voyage, till the grey stony banks were shelving over us, and the wild birch and the willow flung their light wreaths from either side in tangled profusion— now admitting a trembling glimpse of the warm blue sky, and now pierced by a sunset ray, which trailed down some leafy tendril, and shot, like a star, upon the dark stream beneath it. The country rose gradually in the gentle hills which our conductor had described; and our voyage ended where a rude bridge united two mazy pathways, the one leading to a little over- grown hamlet, and the other to the romantic abode which we were seeking.

The charm which had hitherto bound us in silence was now broken by exclamations of wonder and delight. The cottage was, indeed, no less inviting than its description had been. It belonged to people of taste, who had furnished it, inside and out, with every kind of rustic ornament and convenience, and, what was of more importance, it was at our service, together with the peasants who had been left in charge of it.

In less than an hour I had instated my companions in their new home, as comfortably as though they had never known any other, and had procured for myself the state apartment of the little inn, about half a mile distant. Having effected this, we had nothing to do but to sit by the open casement and enjoy the soft breeze, which lent wings to the wild odours of the forest and the music of the neighbouring stream. We sat till long after the sun had gone down, yet still we could not move from our station. The nightingales were beginning their revels, and the old white owl was performing his querulous evolutions, over the waving sheet of golden furze blossoms; the stars, too, were twinkling as if the heavens laughed upon us; and Lucy was flinging her fond arms round the neck of her mother, and wishing that such an hour could last for ever. The journey, however, and the agitations of the day, rendered it necessary for the latter to retire to rest, and I was left for a space with Lucy alone. I fancied that I could perceive the life-blood sporting through her whole frame, and that the pure sensations of joy, which can dispose us to regard with affection those who, at other moments, would be indifferent to us, had more than usually softened her expression towards me. And yet, she was becoming so more and more perfect (for the face never yet was so lovely but it might grow more so by looking on us with kindness), that my spirit sank within me, and ached with the foreboding that the love of such a creature—the love which her nature could only suffer to exist romantic and intense as her beauty—was too much to be the boast of mortal man.

Hope, however, is a hardy plant, for which no soil is too barren, and I had grafted just enough of it upon my despondency to produce a very insupportable crop of doubts. In Lucy's presence I had always been in a tremor : alone, my occupation had been to weigh my deserts, and retire within myself abashed and confounded. On the night of which I speak, the whole multitude of my agitations was alive at once, and the words which might have resolved my uncertainty as to the precise nature of her regard were a thousand times fluttering ineffectually upon my lips. By degrees, however, I took courage from the more than usual sensibility of her mood—from the confidence she reposed in me—from the certainty that my happiness was dear to her. My attempts, perhaps, were not so clear as they might have been, but she had no disposition to misunderstand, for the sake of adding to my embarrassment—she was startled—confused. I had evidently taken her by surprise.

"Can you doubt," she at length said, "that I feel the deepest gratitude—that I consider you my kindest, my best friend? Indeed, I have no other; but had I thousands, I might ask the same. But let the subject drop, I beseech you. I never can leave my mother; therefore, whatever I might confess to you would be of no avail."

Her look, and the earnest tone of her voice, spoke all that was deficient in her words. They dwell upon my recollection, even now, with an unspeakable sensation which is almost too exquisite to be called happiness. That evening! Was it reality? or was it enchantment? I had no leisure to determine, ere Lucy apprized me it was time to depart. She bade me remember that the terms of our intimacy had widely altered : that, for the idle satisfaction of my curiosity, I had sacrificed all the nightingale hours which it would have been difficult to refuse me had I been less encroaching. She was sorry I had rendered it necessary for her to be circumspect, for it was an occupation which she hardly knew how to commence ; nevertheless, she would lose no time in the attempt, and would once more wish me good night.

Three days of perfect bliss melted over us without the dreaded visit from Carrol, to whom we had been compelled to send tidings of our fortune ; and Lucy began her threatened work of circumspection, as though it were merely assumed to give value to the blameless errings and strayings which she knew not how to control. If she denied me the last notes of the nightingale, she listened with me to the first of the lark; and if I was forbidden to talk of love, I was still suffered to press her hand to my heart—to speak of our destinies as though they were already united. There was not a path of our wilderness which had not witnessed some sweet expression—some indescribable look—which seemed to endow me with a fresh capacity for enjoyment. There was not a dimpled circlet of the stream which had not blest me with the downcast blush which would fain have flitted away unseen; not a bank but had contributed its violet to the gift which had perished in her bosom. Every step which I took presented some memorial of yielding resolution, and I would not have exchanged the bliss of my wild heath to be a " bodiless enjoyment " of the blue sky above it.

Alas ! these precious moments were doomed to be of short duration. On the fourth evening, as I was returning to the cottage with Lucy upon my arm, we encountered Mrs. Car-

rol, who was seeking us, with the very unwel-
come news of an invasion from her husband.
He had stood manfully by his castle as long as
it was tenable, and considerably longer than
other folks would have thought it so, in hopes
that the waters would subside and allow him
to estimate the damage which he had sustained.

In these hopes Carrol was at last gratified ;
and his calculation was, that to clear out the
cart-loads of slime which had been washed into
the ground-floor, and to repair the ill- cemented
walls which had never been dry or otherwise than
rotten from the time they were built, together
with the necessity for new doors, new papering,
new furniture, &c., would cost about twice as
much as the famous Mansion of the Moss was
worth—bog, water-rats, and all.   He had consequently left it in the peaceable possession of
the monsters of the mire, and had come to obtain our sympathy in his sufferings, by obliging
us with a very liberal share of them.

Mrs. Carrol had a flush upon her cheek, which
showed that she had been much agitated, and
I thought I could perceive the trace of tears.

Lucy eagerly inquired what more had occurred to disturb her?

"Nothing new," she calmly replied : "Mr. Carrol is in want of means to repair the dilapidations which his property has suffered, and has again been importuning me for my poor Lucy's fortune."

"Then let him have it, I beseech you. It is for my happiness, no less than your's, that he should be satisfied, for, when nothing is left to grant, we may, perhaps, rest in peace."

"No, never, Lucy. My only support has been that you will hereafter enjoy the comforts of which your early days have been so cruelly deprived. Conceive how ineffectual your persuasions must be when my resolution has remained unshaken even by the prospect of —" she paused for a moment, " of parting with you, Lucy."

Lucy repeated the word in dismay. " Does Mr. Carrol dare to contemplate this climax to our misery ? "

"He tells me that the repeated failures in his plans must oblige him to leave the country, unless I concede to his terms of remaining —

that he must go, I know not whither, on fresh speculations, and that you — that you must be left with your friends. Perhaps it is for the best — perhaps."

Indignant as I was at Carrol's villany, I still felt under obligations to him; for the time was surely arrived for the renewal of the conversation which Lucy had forbidden. It was to have been when her mother was happier, and it might now be to save her from increased wretchedness. Lucy's look was consent, and her maiden confusion cast an additional purity and bloom over her beauty, as if to complete the model for a seraph. I need not dwell upon what followed. Mrs. Carrol's sorrows were converted into a gush of joy. She considered me an especial gift of Providence for the protection of her daughter, and declared that she could now cheerfully meet any trial to which she might be exposed. The conversation which had begun in gloom had struck into a gleam of the purest sunshine. There was no dissentient thought amongst us, and before we arrived at the cottage our plan of conduct was completely arranged.

When we entered, Carrol was sitting with

his grim visage sunk deep into his shoulders, his legs extended, and his hands thrust into his pockets. Altogether he looked very much like a man whose occupation was gone, and whose prospects of obtaining another were somewhat precarious. It was no wonder, therefore, if he could afford us but few words of welcome. Our countenances evidently did not bear the expression which he had expected and desired, if we might judge from the dismal appearance of his own. He made a few surly remarks on the water having damaged his map of America, but seemed rather studying how to enter upon the subject of the separation.

"You will be ready," he at last commenced, with a dark look at his wife, "to move in the course of a week or two?"

Mrs. Carrol answered placidly in the affirmative, and he appeared scarcely to know what to make of such cheerful compliance.

"And you have acquainted your daughter with our measures?"

"Fully," said Lucy, with the same serenity.

He felt abashed by her calm, contemptuous manner, and endeavoured to stammer out a sort of apology for the necessity of such plans, with an inquiry as to her future intentions.

"I am not quite certain," she replied, "as to whither my destiny may lead me, but I think it will probably be to America." He looked up with his usual scowl, but averted it again, as though he had encountered a flash of lightning. "You seem surprised, Mr. Carrol," she continued, "but here is a friend who has taken compassion upon the outcast, and, having imbibed from you a taste for draining ponds, is prepared to convey me to the Lake of the Dismal Swamp, or any other desirable neighbourhood your greater experience may lead you to adopt. We can then mutually assist each other in our trade of wills-o'-the-whisp, and I can already perceive what comfort you anticipate from our society."

Mrs. Carrol interfered to preserve the peace by explaining matters in a more methodical style, which, however, her husband did not seem to like much better. We had made a counter speculation which he had not expected, and the only circumstance of it which did not produce a frown was the intended departure of

Lucy to her friends, for the purpose of preparing for her marriage.

" Humph ! " said the cunning man, spreading his map and his elbows upon the table. His thoughts, however, were nearer home than the Blue Mountains, and his face would have made no bad frontispiece to a book of puzzles.

In a day or two, the carriage arrived which was to take Lucy, with a trusty attendant (for Carrol could not lose so good an opportunity of separating her from her mother, who, he insisted, had not strength to accompany her) to London. The morning was chiefly devoted to the anxious and agitated Mrs. Carrol, so that I could seize but a single moment for an unobserved farewell. It was such a one as convinced me that I possessed the whole romantic fervour of her affection, and enriched the prospect of our next meeting with visions too intense to be dwelt upon. Her last words were to remind me that she was only supported in parting from her mother by her confidence that she left a guardian behind who would watch over her with equal solicitude, and to desire the repetition of my promises that I would write to her daily. At length I handed her into the carriage, and she was borne off like the beautiful phantom of a dream.

My engagement to report all that occurred was faithfully performed. I spent the greater part of my time at the cottage, talking over the delights of days to come, and forming plans to counteract every possible manœuvre of Carrol, who had too many cogitations to interfere with us. He had, all of a sudden, hit upon some new speculation, which was too good to be shared, and his mornings, for several days, were employed in nothing but writing letters, and taking them to the post himself. He never said who was his correspondent, but I had accidentally caught a glimpse of the name and address, and noted them down in my memory. In a short time he relieved us of his company altogether, under the pretext of repairing to the nearest seaport to arrange for the voyage to America.

Whether such was really his business, I did not give myself the trouble to inquire, for by this time I had affairs of my own to afford me sufficient employment, and to cause a degree of alarm to which his evil machinations were nothing.

In describing the various friends who had hastened to see her, Lucy had made mention of one respecting whom I had never been able to divest myself of a feeling of jealousy and apprehension. The name of this young man was Walters. In the commencement of his career he had been afflicted with an easy disposition, an inordinate love of pleasure, and means sufficient to tempt those who follow the profession of living upon others to encourage every obliquity of judgment, till his fortune and reputation appeared equally irretrievable. From being the victim we too often become the partner of crime, and Walters had gone on from bad to worse, till he was enrolled amongst the tribe of adventurers who had ruined him. With such characters he had found an easy access to Carrol's house in London, which had been a rendezvous notorious for them, its master being a fellow-labourer in the great web of speculation, and interested in the success of each particular fibre. The careworn appearance of his handsome person, with the remains of a manner which had once been frank and engaging, had distinguished him sufficiently from his companions to obtain a reception which his vanity had been too ready to misunderstand. His heart had taken fire at the attractions of Lucy with all the impetuosity of a nature unaccustomed to restraint; and the subsequent discovery that his own self-abasement was perhaps the cause of his discomfiture had been a species of retribution agonizing in proportion to its justice. As his prospect of success abated, his passion had appeared to gain new strength. His conduct had been wild and desperate. One while he would endeavour to amend and deserve her, and again he would plunge into reckless profligacy in the vain trust of forgetting her. It was at this juncture that Mrs. Carrol's increasing dread of the persons who swarmed about her had compelled her to yield to the rapacity of her husband, and assist him to the possession of his wondrous Wild Water Pond, where, after a few impassioned attempts by letter, Walters had dropped his suit, and had no more been heard of. Three years had now elapsed, and he appeared before Lucy, as he gave her to understand, in every thing but his love an altered man. As soon as her absence had suffered his frenzy to settle down, and left him to the fair exercise of his reason, he had determined upon adopting new courses, and one day trying his fate under better auspices. For this purpose, he had quitted his evil companions, which was easily enough to be done when they had fleeced him of every thing, and had tried his best to turn what talents he possessed to a worthy account. He had tried, and had prospered, and now the meed for which he had laboured was irrecoverably lost to him. Nevertheless, he would learn to bend to his fate, and only petitioned to witness, as a friend, the happiness which he could partake no otherwise.

Such was the account with which Walters had excited Lucy's sympathy, and which I could not help thinking exceedingly incredible. It was a mere deception, I felt, to procure opportunities for a last effort, and I could see him with my mind's eye endeavouring to supplant me with a tale of hypocritical meekness, which made me writhe with apprehension. I raked up every word that she had formerly said of his person and his talents, and each recollection contributed to make him more dreaded. I convinced myself that she had rejected him merely on account of his profligacy, and that his reformation, whether real or assumed, would put her upon making comparisons, which could not fail of telling to my disadvantage. My blood was in a tumult, and I was upon the point of writing to entreat that she would never see him again. But, then, what would Lucy say to my mistrust of her? What would my own pride hereafter say to the recollection that I had been obliged to supplicate the dismissal of a rival? No! let Walters do his worst. If Lucy's inclinations led her from me, I would bear it as I could. It was a good touchstone whereon to try the strength of her affection, and if she returned still faithful, she would be a greater prize than ever.

At last the day arrived which was to bring Lucy's self to resolve all my doubts. With what an anxious tremour did I watch the road she was to come! How eagerly did I pace it backwards and forwards, and strain my eyes for a sight of the carriage. The sun had set, and yet she came not. I continued at my station long after the shades had set in, conjuring up sounds which only lived in my fancy, or only proceeded from the beating of my heart. Lucy was absent still. It was not till late in the night that I returned to the cottage, where Mrs. Carrol was still sitting up in expectation. My appearance sufficiently indicated the disturbed state of my mind, but what consolation could she offer? Lucy's arrangements might not have been completed—her friends might have protracted her stay—a thousand circumstances might have occurred, which she would, no doubt, explain satisfactorily when we met. But why had she not written? All our reasonings were destroyed by this unanswerable question, and I determined to seek a solution by the readiest means. I would set off to London myself.

By sunrise I was on my way. I will not detain the reader with all the agony of a long journey, with all the inquiries I made upon the road, and with all the disappointments I encountered. It was nearly midnight when I entered London. Of the objects around me I saw nothing but a moving chaos; or, if my perception was for a moment more particularly excited, it was only when some impediment crossed my way to heighten my impatience.

At length I reached the door of Lucy's friends. I knocked. Oh, how I remember— how I feel, even now whilst I am telling it— the harrowing, suffocating sensation with which I waited to be admitted! My first question may be supposed. The servant *had not heard* how Lucy was. She had returned home ten days ago. I started as though my heart-strings had snapped asunder. He stared with sur- prise, as did the family when I was ushered in. They could give me no farther information, and had been under much alarm at not having re- ceived accounts of her safe arrival.

There was but one question more to com- plete the measure of my agony, but I knew not how to ask it. — I knew not how to sully the resplendent vision which Lucy must have left upon their minds, by breathing a doubt that she could act unworthy of herself. It was not till we had run over all the chances which might have impeded her journey — till we had satisfied ourselves that she must be detained on the road by illness, (a circumstance of which, as matters stood, I would have given my existence to be assured), that I ventured to mention the name of Walters. I saw that my suspicion had been anticipated. Her friends looked upon each other in dismay, and then with one accord declared that it was impossible —it was out of the question ; that was to say, it was not at all likely that Lucy should have so far forgotten herself. The faintness of their contradiction wrought me to a frenzy. I forgot the discretion with which I had concealed my evil forebodings. I besought them to imagine all that I could ask of them, and then listened with ghastly patience to all the particulars they could give me.

In a word, though Lucy's manner had never given them reason to suspect that she entertained an undue regard for Walters, they were bound to confess that he had called to see her upon alleged business the day before her departure, which had, as it seemed, been much accelerated by the circumstance. She had not told them what had transpired, but it was evidently something by which she had been strongly agitated.

This was all I could learn from them, and, in a few moments, I was again rushing along the streets.

I have before mentioned that I had accidentally seen the address of one of Carrol's letters. It was to Walters, and I glided along in spirit-like rapidity till I stood before the house. The neighbourhood was wretched and deserted; nothing was stirring to break the distant din of the more busy world, and the street was lighted only by two or three dim lamps, as though it were especially devoted to persons and practices most congenial to darkness.

The door was opened by a miserable creature of all work, who at first denied that any such person as Walters lived there; but my necessity for seeing him was too great to stand upon trifles, and I obtained an answer more to my satisfaction, by announcing myself as Mr. Carrol. The servant apologised for not having known me, and had taken so many letters with my address to the post, that there was no doubt I might be shown up. What could be meant by this mystery? Was I to find Walters alone, or—— I did not dare to conclude the sentence, even in thought.

He *was* alone, and the trepidation of our meeting was mutual.

" Who are you?" he exclaimed, turning deadly pale, and gazing upon me as though I had been a spectre. I could not answer. There was a volume of strange things swelling in my bosom, which struggled to be uttered all at once. I could not move, lest I should tear him piecemeal before I had examined the lineaments which had displaced me in the heart of Lucy.

I have him before me with an identity vivid and aching as an evil conscience. He was handsome, as he had been described, but his features had more the character of dissimulation than intellect. His dress was in the extreme of fashion, but his general stamp was that of the pretender.

" Who are you?" he again cried, with increased agitation. My sight grew sick as I gazed on him, my mind more wild in the imagination of all that could annihilate it ; and

I breathed my name with a groan, as though it were the confession of some burning shame. He appeared relieved, professed to know nothing about me, and begged to hear my business.

The plea of ignorance, however, did not serve him long; and he then found it expedient to shelter himself from my questions, by taking the excitement under which I was labouring as an excuse for the singular intrusion.

"Upon my word, sir," he continued, with an easy and lazy flow of language, which brought the withering conviction that he had nothing to apprehend from me; "if you are one of the numerous suitors of Miss ———, I should think you sufficiently apprized of her change of mind, by the necessity for making these inquiries. You, of course, know very well that she would have accepted *any one* who could enable her to follow her mother to America; and if, out of the many, she has decided upon giving the preference to me, pray allow me to assure you that constancy is a mere country virtue; and that a glance at the fashionable world will show it so little prized, that you will scarcely think your fate worth lamenting. Nothing will give me greater pleasure than to show every attention to a gentleman in whose commendation I have heard Miss —— speak so highly, and if you are in town for any time, and will do me the favour of a call to-morrow, or next day, I have no doubt I can give you introductions which will make your time pass agreeably. At present, I have an engagement in the West End, for which I am obliged to beg you will excuse me."

The superb coolness of all this had an effect rather opposite to the one intended, for I could not doubt that he took me for some love-lorn village swain whose wits were as simple as his feelings, and thought that he had nothing to do but to abash me by carrying matters with a high hand. If anything could have raised me to a higher pitch of desperation, it was the feeling that such must have been Lucy's description of me.

" Hold, sir," I replied, rising up at the same time with him, and preparing myself for any extremity; " your friends in the West

End must excuse you for to-night, for if I have seemed paralyzed at the easy assurance with which you treat this matter, it has not been from the want of wherewithal to talk about. That Miss ——— is subjected for the present to very painful surmises, I will not dispute, but it is possible that she is misrepresented. Therefore, without asking further questions, I will simply trouble you to inform me where she is to be found, in order that I may have the history of her change from her own lips. Refuse me, and her mysterious disappearance is ground enough for an appeal where you may chance to be more communicative. We do not part without trying the alternative."

I had observed that all I said produced little effect, until I made the allusion to justice, and this caused a nervous tremor which convinced me that he had something to dread from it. I followed up the fortunate hit with a determination from which he had no escape, and which assured him that his vague and insulting offhandedness was out of the question. I told him of his being denied by the servant of the house, and pointed out to him his portmanteau half packed up for flight. These were slight charges to alarm him, but, aided apparently by an accuser within, they brought him to terms much sooner than I could have imagined. He acknowledged that his engagement to the West End was invented to spare me the mortification of farther discussion, regretted that Lucy was to be subjected to importunities from which she had taken such pains to retire, and, with a cool consciousness of success, invited me to share a conveyance which he had even then in waiting to take him to Wild Water Pond.

"Lucy at Wild Water Pond! That place of which she has so much horror!"

"It appears, sir, that there are other things of which she has had a greater horror. But since we are to be fellow-travellers for so long a journey, it were best to drop all subjects of annoyance, till I am in a situation to give you more satisfactory answers."

The proposal had reason in it. We descended into the street, found the vehicle at the appointed place, and, having nothing to impede

our passage, got clear of London in a few
minutes.

My companion, who had been looking un-
easily to the right and left as we passed the
streets, (although it was nearly daybreak, and
no one was to be seen) now entered carelessly
into conversation, and affected to forget that
there was any cause of enmity between us.
Alas! such a manner did far more to shake my
confidence in Lucy, than any assertions he
could have made. It seemed incompatible with
any thing but certainty, and he had skill
enough to perceive that such was my conclusion. From one light subject he rambled on to
another, in the hope that I might grow tho-
roughly discouraged, and give up my project
before the journey's end. But I had another
project behind, upon which he had not calculated. Be the event what it might, I had been
injured past the power of forgiveness. It was
my fixed resolve that the moment I had seen
Lucy, and either reproached her with her falsehood, or asked pardon for my doubts, her fame
should be avenged, or her fault punished, in
the cold blood of my rival. The work of re-

flection was too excruciating—I banished it forcibly. Happily, the weight upon my brain, with the fatigue which I had undergone, at last gave me a relief something between sleep and stupefaction.

By the time the country began to assume the features of the Wild Water regions, the sun had set. The horizon was hidden by a long blue bank of mist, softening delicately into a deep orange reflection of the departed orb, which, in its turn, melted into a lucid, watery blue. A long, lazy river wound, glowing like gold, through the monotonous grey of the flag-fields, and straggling clumps of alders, and the whole was enlivened only by flocks of geese and a few starved cattle.

In this scene we came to a spot where the road branched off, and an old broken handpost intimated that the rest of our journey was to be performed on foot. Soon it became quite dark, and the damp and foggy atmosphere, with the screams of the herons, and the unwholesome effluvia of the green ooze, assured me that we were approaching near to Carrol's domains.

At this juncture we perceived the dim halo round a cabin light. It conducted us to the abode of one of those forlorn beings who lived by taking wild fowl, and it was fortunate that we stopped there, for all land communication with the country in that direction had been cut off, ever since Carrol had let the river into the bog. I learnt, moreover, that the old people of the Lock House had been removed, punts and all, to the Mansion, which, for some reason or other, had of late only been accessible by signal, on which occasions a boat was sent out. This mode of proceeding would not answer my purpose, and I besought our informant to suggest other means of approaching it. He had nothing, he said, but a small shooting skiff, which only held two persons, and it was impossible to direct us how to paddle ourselves three miles in so dark a night. It will, however, be readily supposed that I was not to be dissuaded from the attempt, and Walters was so completely disconcerted by my continued firmness, that he offered no opposition. We stepped into the shallop, and my knowledge of the swamp was not so bad but I steered our course, in spite of all the dangerous obstacles, directly towards the Mansion of the Moss.

My suspense was now, in a few moments, to be ended. We stepped on shore without speaking a word, and proceeded to the house like two deadly foes to the lists. Late as it was, we found the hall door open ; the floods, indeed, had warped it so as to prevent the possibility of its closing. The drawing-room, likewise, stood stubbornly ajar, and suffered us to force our way through without so much as a creak.

As we entered, I perceived the apartment to be partially lighted by a smouldering wood-fire. We stopped by mutual impulse. At the opposite sides sat two figures engaged in a conversation so exciting that our entrance was unobserved.

"And you refuse to let me depart ?" said the electric voice of Lucy, with its most indignant energy.

"If you are in such a hurry to depart, I should be glad to know why you came ?" replied the brutal tones of Carrol. "You cannot say that I brought you ? "

"No—you did not use violence, it is true.

—You employed means still more base—you instructed your confederate in London to show me a pretended confidential letter, describing my mother's secret removal to this horrid place, in order to our separation. You knew that I could not hesitate in following, and thus made the feelings of nature, which a savage would have respected, the cause perhaps of my lasting misery. Have you not deprived me of all possibility of escape?"

"You can depart with Walters, whenever he chooses to fetch you."

"You know he dare not see me. You know he is fully aware of my utter contempt for him; or, if he is not, you have misled him by false statements."

I had heard enough, and was in the act of springing forward to clasp her once more to my heart, but Walters eagerly held me back, as if he would learn more.

"I grant you," returned Carrol, with a wrathful grin, "that it requires some courage to face such a born devil, but Walters will be here nevertheless, and I should advise you to receive him in the light I propose; for this is a lonely place, and, you understand, I am the master." He paused and clenched his teeth, and again grinned horribly.

" So, Mr. Carrol, you threaten to murder me ? Oh, for some new invented words to express my scorn ! Yet, I thank you for this liberal and complete display of your virtues, for my poor unhappy mother must now dismiss her last scruple, and leave you to your career of wickedness alone."

" Think you so ? You have come here to seek *her*, and why may *she* not come to seek *you* ? I should be sorry for such a necessity, for you know the air of this place does not agree with her. Come, come, let us talk reason—Walters is a man of the world—and an old friend ; and has taken a liking to you, for which nothing short of the devil can account. As for this new acquaintance whom you talk of marrying, who is he, and what is he, but a dull-witted piece of common-place, who will make his way in life about as glibly as he would flounder through this cursed mud-pond ? You take him because he promises to take you to America ; why, so will Walters—that I promise you faithfully. He *must* go to America, whether he likes it or not ; for, just to give you an idea of his strange infatuation for you, he has thought it worth his while to find me the equivalent to the means which your obstinate mother re- fused me, and must leave the country as soon as he can."

" A felon ! your consideration for my hap- piness is really beyond praise. Mr. Walters commits felony to offer you a bribe to sacrifice me, and I am to enjoy his society in America, whilst you bring my mother to the Mansion of the Moss to enjoy your respectable acquisi- tion ! It was unnecessary to tell me this. It proves your head to be as bad as your heart —and the only alternative I have is to be mur- dered !"

Carrol's rage could be curbed no longer, and burst forth in appalling execrations. He jumped from his seat with a stamp that might have beaten in the rotten flooring, and my com- panion advanced a step with me in expectation of some act of desperate violence. He, how- ever, only seized the poker, and plunged it into the slumbering fire, as though it had been the heart of the undaunted Lucy. The flame sprang up bright and high; and, when he turned to glare destruction upon his helpless victim, he encountered the poised figures and concentrated fury of his unexpected visiters. Lucy shrieked and sprang to meet me, whilst Walters, thrilling to the quick with disappointment and the astounding conviction of the extent to which he had been duped, flung himself like a tiger upon his false confederate, and, had his strength been equal to his rage, would have strangled him on the spot. Carrol, with the supernatural exertions of terror, contrived to extricate himself, and rushed out of the door, pursued closely by his determined assailant. I let them have the dispute to themselves, and cared not how soon they destroyed each other. Shouts and curses apprized us that they were again in contact, and Lucy clung to me in a convulsion of horror.

"Is it thus that you repay my interest?" articulated the struggling voice of Carrol.

"Is it thus I find her love, which you called so devoted to me?" replied the infuriated Walters.

" Have I deserved to be murdered ? "

" Have I forfeited my life to be duped ? "

" Part them—for God's sake, part them ! " cried the shuddering, the forgiving, Lucy.

She spoke too late.   A heavy plunge in the water announced that they had parted of themselves, and that Carrol had made the attempt to escape by swimming.

" A light ! a light ! " cried Walters, rushing back to the room, and vanishing with a brand from the fire.   Nothing would suit him but extermination, and we followed to withhold him, attended by the few alarmed and forlorn domestics, amongst whom was the decrepid old man of the Lock.

" It is useless," said he—" useless to think of swimming through this slime to the towing-path.   The boat ! the boat ! "

All the boats we could find were immediately pushed off with lights—Walters being with difficulty restrained from pursuing his vengeance to the last.   It was very dark and foggy, and the brands and the lanterns only threw their glare to the distance of a few feet. We watched their dim meteor-like courses to and fro, without success, for a breathless half hour. At last, one of the lights stopped, and a shout informed us that Carrol was found. A few moments more, and the boat glided slowly towards the shore—the two who had gone forth with it gazing with fixed horror at the burthen which lay at the bottom.

When we came to behold, there was indeed a frightful sight, not the less thrilling from the unexpected performance of a sentence which I had often sportively pronounced to be the most appropriate. Stark stiff, and scarcely to be distinguished from the filth of the morass, the body of Carrol bore witness that his soul had passed away to a land whither his speculations had tended but too little. To lament was impossible. We could but turn shuddering away, and trust fervently that such punishment might be sufficient to efface the guilt which had led to it.

I looked round to see if the resentment of Walters had ceased with that of the weeping Lucy and myself, but he was gone. Having no longer his rage to support him, the shame of his discomfiture had doubtless rendered him unable to sustain our presence.   He had stepped into one of the boats, and escaped in the midst of our consternation ; and the justice which pursued him was eluded equally.   I never heard of him but once afterwards, and that was in a newspaper account of his having landed at New York.

In a few weeks from this time, the visions of Lucy's young ambition were realized.   She became the mistress of her mother's home——the blissful guardian of smiles which she had despaired of again beholding ; and, if she lavished the reflection of them upon one who knew not how to deserve her, she was contented to think that what was wanting in merit was amply made up in boundless devotion.

THE PIC-NIC.

I gaed a waefu' gate yestreen.
Burns.

"What on earth," I exclaimed, on the hottest of the dog days, "can move mortal men and women to leave their lemonade and ices behind their cool veranda-blinds and toil through pigeon-pies on the top of a hill in such a Phœnix-frying sun as this?"

Such was the mood in which I received an invitation to a pic-nic party, in which, nevertheless, I was enlisted in spite of myself. I would not have it supposed, however, that the reasoning of *man* could have brought me to this impious defiance of Apollo's wrath.——No; the tempter was in petticoats——and such a one!——I was sitting in the draft between two windows——

With outstretch'd legs, loose neckcloth, fluttering frill,
Fanning my bosom with my tailor's bill——

I beg pardon for the poetry, but when I think

of that dark-eyed maid my pen always runs riot—I was sitting with two tumblers before me, the one containing lemonade, the other camomile tea, which I sipped alternately for the more complete enjoyment of their sweets and bitters, when she overwhelmed me by demanding—"Is it true you are not going with us?"

There is something to me so bewitching in the graceful bend of maiden symmetry, something so persuasive in the blush and the smile of a naturally pale and pensive countenance, something so totally irresistible in the soft tone which is struggling with reluctant bashfulness —————— I see how it will be—I shall be at my rhymes again presently—"Go with you!" cried I—"ay, to the world's end!—how shall we travel?"

"There are three jaunting cars," replied my beauty, "and there are only eighteen of us, and there are only five gentlemen, twelve others having excused themselves in consideration of their complexions, and we have only fifteen miles to go, and we shall only be out nine or ten hours." I could not help gasping for breath as I rejoined, on hearing the place of our destination, that it was *only* up hill all the way, and a car had *only* one horse, which would *only* be a hack, and would *only* knock up before we could reach the second mile-stone. Nevertheless, I was bound to

> " Do as was my duty ;
> Honour the shadow of her shoe-tie,"

and follow her to the world's end, as aforesaid."

The party being arranged, the remainder of the day was devoted to squeezing lemons, corking bottles, and writing bills of fare—mirth, bustle, and expectation, danced in our ladies' eyes like cupids on a holyday, and I thought the toils of preparation could scarcely be inferior to those of the undertaking itself— " Hillo," cries a dashing captain from the assembled group of the F——'s and the B——'s and the P——'s, " bring here that carouser on camomile tea."

" My dear sir, the thing is impossible ! for every drop that I squeezed out of those hard-hearted lemons I should indubitably break a blood-vessel—you see I am relaxed to perfect imbecility."

My expostulations were all in vain; and in spite of my decided opinion that there was no more mercy in the monster than " milk in a male tiger," I was dragged off and condemned to something worse than the galleys in the housekeeper's room, for I was given to understand that one of the chief pleasures on occasions like the present is to play the part of your servants, and do your duty in that station of life in which it has pleased your friends to call you. My duty (I blush to name it) was (in kind consideration of the intense heat, and my consequent inability for corporeal exertion) to make sundry little delicacies by a fire three feet long and about two feet in height; and the duty of the personage I was expected to rival was to stand by and poke it—I saved my character but I ruined my constitution.

At length the day—" the great, the important day, big with the fate" of three hack steeds and eighteen goodly personages, burst through my window-curtains. I had coaxed myself to sleep on the preceding night with the *possibility that it was not impossible* that it might rain, seeing that all sublunary things are subject to change, and that the earth had now been baked for upwards of six weeks — but I was disappointed. Phœbus was in finer feather than ever, and the little girls were dancing over my head with the most heart-rending gaiety—nevertheless, I was a philosopher, and resolved to stand by my promise with magnanimity. I broke my fast with a glass of camomile tea, which gave me vigour to dispose of a bowl of strawberries and cream, and tilted at the most accomplished jokers of the party.

The breakfast was scarcely over when we were attracted to the window by a strange, outlandish noise, resembling the gambols of sweeps on May-day, or the more musical clink of marrow-bones and cleavers. I had scarce time to exclaim " What the deuce is that ! " when I beheld three vehicles approaching the house at the instigation of certain animals which I should, without doubt, have taken for crocodiles, had I not been assured by the captain that they were very excellent horses. All our souls and bodies were in instant commotion—

the ladies donned their bonnets, and seized their parasols, while the gentlemen rushed out to the stowing of the cargo :——hampers and baskets and bundles passed to and fro with a rapidity that was truly fearful, and threatened to flatten some of the handsomest noses of the party. I am well assured that I was considered a very helpless sort of a person, for, in truth, I was more occupied in getting out of the way than in contributing my exertions to the general weal. I suspect, likewise, that my skill in the commissariat department was but lightly esteemed, for, when I hinted at taking a shower-bath with us, the proposal was absolutely considered as a joke.

At last there was a general cry for the passengers. The captain mounted the dickey of the best equipage, and was soon accommodated with five of the lightest insides ;——his friend the cornet made ready with equal alacrity, and, to my dismay, I was informed that I, even I, was to be the charioteer of the third. At the same time (I confess it with gratitude) I received a confidential communication that it would not be incumbent upon me to show any uncommon degree of Olympic spirit, as I had been appointed *conducteur* to the married ladies and the crockery-ware, purposely that I might not want an excuse for arriving two hours after the others. Five married ladies and all the crockery-ware! And what to draw them? Oh, ye Gods! my blood curdled at the sight; I could have picked a better horse out of the maws of the ravens! Such a ewe-necked, raw-boned, rat-tailed, broken-kneed, mallendered, sallandered, spavined, and string-halted skeleton never entered the precincts of a dog-kennel. The owner, however, assured me, upon the honour of a gentleman, that it could see very tolerably with one eye, and had the best wind of any horse in the country.

I had applied four or five thwacks with the whip, and had begun to expect that my quadruped would shortly agree to follow his companions, who were now almost out of sight, when the operation was suspended by a shout in the distance, and the appearance of a corpulent gentleman in leather breeches and boots, with a bundle at his back.

" Oh, here's Mr. D!" cried the ladies, all

at once. "I knew he would come," said one; "How kind!" cried another; "How he runs!" exclaimed a third—and I must, in justice, declare that, for a gentleman whose legs diverged like a pair of compasses, and who lacked some of the wind for which my horse was so celebrated, he wagged along with very praiseworthy rapidity.——"How d'ye do, Mr. D?" cried all at once.

Mr. D. wiped his red face and powdered head, and panted sorely—"Servant, ladies—pooff—oh dear!—pooff—how hot it is—only just got your note—pooff—came off at a moment's warning—pooff—ran like a lamplighter—dear me, dear me—brought my share of the pic-nic though—round of beef—fat as I am—all melted, I'm afraid, and—beg pardon, young gentleman—permit me to put it between your legs."

" Ye Gods, ye Gods ! must I endure all this ?"

The reeking bundle was placed under my nose, and Mr. D. ascended the after-part of the car. The shafts rose, and the belly-band tightened, and I was very near leaping from my station under the idea that Mr. D. and the horse intended playing at *see-saw*, or rather that the latter was to be hoisted over my head and seated in the laps of the ladies. The event, however, not occurring, I resumed the application of the whip, and had the satisfaction of seeing my animal set up his back and grind away beyond my hopes.

Oh, how I wish my limits would permit me to dilate upon the dust and the heat; the stoppages and the walkings up hill; the jokes of Mr. D. and the applauses of the ladies. For be it known that Mr. D. was something of a wit, and very much of a roysterer, and, altogether, a very desirable companion—when there was room for him. One thing I must not omit to state, which is that no person whatsoever should judge of a horse by appearances, or mistrust his own abilities before he has given them a fair trial. We overtook the cars which preceded us, and, had it not been for the screams of the married ladies and the clattering of the dishes, I verily and truly believe we could have beaten them.—Mr. D. thought so too, for which I honour him.

We now arrived within sight of our destination, and I found my spirits not a little exhilarated at the prospect of being once more upon my legs. Perhaps this happy state of mind may have been in some measure owing to the consciousness of having proved myself a worthy candidate for gymnastic honours; but it was more likely to arise from a sweet smile of my dark-eyed maid, who beckoned me to approach her car, and assured me, that, since I was evidently the most accomplished knight, she had determined to place herself under my protection for the rest of the expedition.

With such a prospect, I leaped to the ground as lightly as if my joints had not once been shaken out of the sockets. The captain took care of the hacks, (which, without dispute, must have been nearly related to the horses of the sun, or, they must, many miles ago, have sunk beneath his beams) the cornet saw to the unloading of the baggage, and I did my best to play the agreeable to thirteen petticoats; for Mr. D. was dusting himself amongst the butter-cups, and another young gentleman, whom I have not mentioned, was too much enthralled by an individual enchantress to be worth the notice of the rest. It would be an uncourtly breach of confidence were I to relate all the gentle things that were said to me. Let it suffice that I had interest to procure, by general assent, a total manumission from the labours of the day, and received the fairest arm in the world, with strict injunctions to make myself as happy as I could.

" And now," said my dark-eyed maid, " are you still sorry that you came with us ? "

" Say no more of it," I replied ; " I would come every day of my life, if I lived to the age of Methuselah."

Of course eating and drinking (plebeian vices !) were the first amusements which occurred to the earthly minds of such of our gentles as did not happen to be favourites with the ladies—that is, *very especial ones*—I mean —in short, the reader knows I mean a delicate allusion to myself. We stood upon the summit of a hill, reconnoitering the valley for an appropriate scene of carousal. Huge cliffs on the opposite side extended their delicious shadows over the green bosom of the wood, and the blue streamlet looked cool as the springs of Lapland.

"Delightful!" ejaculated Mr. D., who had just risen from the grass with a pair of green buck-skins; "let us carry down the provisious without more ado. The two dragoons shall bring the two hampers, the clergyman carry the baskets, and I my own beef."—With that he flourished the saturated bundle, and pushed boldly at the declivity.

Alas and alas! the hill was steep and the grass was slippery! poor Mr. D. lost his feet and his bundle at the same instant. The whole party set up a shout, and down he rolled—I never saw a man turn over at such a rate in my life, and I am quite convinced that he would have distanced the best roller at Greenwich fair. The beef was inspired with a noble emulation, and contended the race most magnanimously. Bets ran high; and the odds varied from two to one on the man to five to four on the beef. The wager, however, was not doomed to be decided, for Mr. D., in throwing his arms about for some kind friend to stop his career, unhappily seized upon his competitor, and they both plunged into the river together; which the captain pronounced to be a *dead heat.*

At first there was some alarm for the consequences of this surprising feat; but, on Mr. D.'s emerging, like a river god, from the bed of the stream, and waving his hat, which had gone toddling after him, our hearts beat more freely and our youths commenced the removal of the goods; something cautioned in their motions by the fearful example which had just been exhibited. Mr. D. made the best of his way to a farm-house — I heard him churning the water in his boots at the distance of a hundred yards.

We formed our head-quarters in a small green space which was nearly insulated by the brook; a world of weeping birch and feathering ash trembled over our heads, and beneath our feet smiled the sweetest cowslips that ever welcomed the happy to scenes of happiness.—I never before saw man so free from mortal care, or woman so like an angel. While the gentlemen who did not happen to be favourites with the ladies (meaning, as I said before, all but myself and the luckless Mr. D.) were emancipating whole hecatombs of the barn-door population, with certain quarrelsome bottles of champagne which had been threatening to break each other's heads almost from the commencement of the journey, I made myself useful in spreading cloaks and coats, for our more delicate companions to recline upon. Never was a bank so daintily adorned — I sat upon the same cloak with the dark eyes, and could have spouted extemporaneous poetry till

" Scott, Rogers, Moore, and all the better brothers,"

had hid their diminished heads and looked aghast. What a time for philosophy ! " Alas !'' thought I, " that these smooth, transparent foreheads and slender forms should ever be furrowed by the cares of matrimony, or bowed down by the toils of nursing ! How many of these delicate creatures will, probably, ere another twelvemonth elapses, become the property of surly dogs who will repel the infatuated glances of philosophers like me with the jealousy of a mastiff growling over a mutton-chop ! How many will look pensively back upon this scene of merriment, and wish, and vainly wish, for the same freedom of spirit, the same lightness of heart, the same retrospections, and the same buoyant confidence in the future ! ''

I was getting from pensive to sad, and from sad to sorry, with a rapidity which would very soon have affected the fountains of mine eyes, when I was roused by a peal of light laughter, to which the sonorous " Ho, ho, ho ! " of Mr. D. beat time like the drum in a band of music. He made his appearance in a smock-frock, worsted stockings, and hob nails, and challenged to roll down again with any gentleman or lady of the party, and give them half way. The gauntlet not being taken up, (though I am not sure but I saw a pair of little black eyes very much inclined to sparkle with defiance) he wheeled round and made a dead point at a magnificent venison pasty, which rose up from the midst of the subordinate building like the tower of Babel. Turret after turret disappeared, the chickens were dissected, the pies evaporated, and the champagne banged like a battery upon the scene of slaughter.

"Another slice," quoth Mr. D., "with a little of the jelly and some of the under crust—thank'e — Ladies, your health — Ho, ho, ho! what a roll it was! I'll be bound I made the turf as smooth as a bowling green, and flattened every stone in my course. Happy to take a glass with you, sir — I mean the gentleman in the blue cravat—So, so — that beats arquebusade and opodeldoc too — cured all my bruises in a crack — I never use any other embrocation than champagne—Another slice, please—with a little more of the jelly — *sicut antea*, as the doctors say—Harkee," continued he, flinging his arm round my neck, and whispering while he was masticating two square inches of venison, which made some of the party believe he was devouring my ear, "how do you think I got this doublet and hose? I knew my leathers would only be fit for spindles after their sousing, and so I made a swap with the farmer — ho, ho, ho! I'll sell you my smock at half-price."

By this time the lovers had stolen away, and the ladies were anxious to embark on their voyages of discovery. Mr. D. reluctantly wiped his mouth, the soldiers finished their stirrup cup, and the party paired off upon their various expeditions. I led my dark-eyed companion along the most sequestered path I could discover, and would not exchange the remembrance of that brief hour for any ten years of any hero upon record.

" Indeed ! " says the captain, " and what might have been the subject of your conversation ? "

" Sir, it was such as you might have taken for a model, and would have cheered the very heart of your grandmother. I urged no suit but that the nature and innocence which then hallowed her path might pass unchanged through life's vicissitudes, and I expected no gratification beyond the simple promise that what I most praised in her should be most valued by her. At that moment, I could scarce number the arguments which might have been produced to prove to the satisfaction of all

·· ————cavaliers of twenty-five or thirty,"

how far inferior, in true pleasure, is the light conquest of woman's heart, to the blest remembrance of having guided her steps to happiness.

> Our path was by the river's side,
>   The voice of mirth had ceased to sound,
> The sunbeam, in its vesper pride,
>   Showed nought but solitude around.

Well done, my muse — but that is enough for the present — you are getting troublesome. The scene described in the stanza was so very appropriate for a pair of lovers, that I really felt an inconceivable load off my mind when I found the advantages had not been disregarded. On turning an abrupt angle, I beheld the clergyman whispering honeyed words into his lady's ear, and both of them, apparently, ascending into the third heaven of lovers as fast as Mr. D. had rolled down into the river. My hardhearted companion was on the point of making known our near neighbourhood, but I motioned her to silence, and led her off upon tip-toe, congratulating myself on my narrow escape from a breach of Love's code, which would have hung heavy upon my conscience for ever afterwards. I had no sooner entered a fresh path, however, than I was threatened with a calamity of precisely the same nature, by the Captain and another of our beauties ; and in a third direction I almost stumbled upon the bosom secrets of the ferocious Cornet.

My dark-eyed friend seemed amused by my embarrassment, but I could not help insinuating a serious degree of mortification that no one should have informed me of the customs usually observed on these occasions, for I was as ready to fall in love as any one else, had I known it to be necessary. I considered that the least she could do was to protect my character from the aspersions of the discontented, and repute me the author of all the soft things that had been reserved for the next occasion. Being assured that I had no cause for alarm, I regained presence of mind enough to look about me, lest I should intrude upon Mr. D. and her mother. But Mr. D. was of too ample dimensions to fall to the lot of one individual. The married ladies chose to share his attractions amongst them, and he met us, like a stag of ten, in the van of his herd.

It was now time to harness the hacks, and while this operation was in performance I could plainly distinguish the slayers of men discoursing in terms very derogatory to my skill as a whip. This I instantly set down for envy, for I had almost beaten them with the worst horse and the heaviest load (to say nothing of Mr. D. as supercargo,) and I was quite certain that now the pies were eaten and the above gentlemen exchanged for my beauty, I could win the race home with ease. I started, as before, the last of the three, husbanding the powers of my crocodile with laudable jockeyship. The night became very dark, and we were only aware of our relative distances by the rattle of our wheels and the merciless cracking of our whips. My opponents were evidently gaining ground upon me, and my passengers were beginning to grow clamorous, under the idea that we should lag too far behind, and so be robbed and murdered.

I believe I have hinted in various places that I am endowed with a certain portion of that greatest of all earthly goods called philosophy, and it was this which enabled me to calculate the chances in my favour with a precision that rendered me deaf to the remonstrances of persons who were less gifted. In the first place, it was granted on all sides that we were going down hill ; and in the next, it was not to be denied that every one of our quadrupeds, from the testimony of his knees, was wofully addicted to stumbling. Now I had always considered it as an axiom that a horse was more likely to tumble down hill than up hill, and that an overdriven one had no sort of conscience whatever. Consequently it was incumbent on me to use all proper circumspection, seeing that I had six ladies and all the dishes to answer for, besides a seventh person whom etiquette forbids me to mention.

The caution which I had adopted was equally necessary for my competitors, and, since they were cursed with too much courage to follow it, the chances were about fifty to one that one of them would measure his length upon the ground. The other must, of course, pull up to assist his comrade, and in this dilemma I had settled it with my high-mettled skeleton that we should politely wish them good night.

I believe it was about mid-way that my cal-

culations were verified.   I first heard a crash,
then a general scream, then the word of command to halt, and afterwards the jolly " Ho, ho,
ho ! " of Mr. D., which gave me the satisfactory intelligence that my enemies had come to
a downfall, and that none of the party had experienced bodily injury.

Now was the time for my triumph, but I
must say I bore it like a hero.   I was beginning an admonitory harangue with " I told you
how it would be," when the sight of their
distress completely disarmed me.   The noble
steed still lay panting upon the ground, while
the captain cut the harness to pieces for his
liberation : the two shafts had snapped off
like sticks of barley-sugar, and the whole ma-
chinery appeared to have received a shock
irreparable.

" How shall we get home ? " cried the distressed heroines ; " we cannot sleep under the
hedge."

" Beg pardon, ladies," replied Mr. D., " it
is one of the most comfortable ditches I was
ever pitched into — I went right in upon my
head and received no manner of damage, ex-

cepting a tug of the pigtail which hung in a bramble, and a few thorns which took advantage of the absence of my buck-skins."

My heart melted within me, and I agreed with the opposition carrier that if he would convey the vanquished champion and the ponderosity of Mr. D., I would endeavour to persuade my horse to accommodate the five forlorn damsels. The proposal was thankfully agreed to. The fragments of the wreck were removed to the road-side, the miserable hack turned into the first field that presented itself, and I finished the remainder of the journey with eleven ladies and not a single accident.

Having thus immortalized myself in my debut in pic-nics, I must inform my reader, in confidence, that I never intend to risk the laurels which were so hardly obtained; for, independently of a notion which still haunts me that both the warriors are *in reality* much better whips than myself, and that the next opportunity would make it appear, I suffered so excessively from fear, anxiety, broiling, and dislocation, that I lay for many days under serious apprehensions of a consumption; and

CHATELAR.

He would wait the hour
When her lamp lightened in the tower;
'Twas something yet, if, as she pass'd,
Her shade was o'er the lattice cast.
SCOTT.

THERE are no mysteries into which we are so
fond of diving as the mysteries of the heart.
The hero of the best novel in the world, if he
could not condescend to fall in love, might
march through his three volumes and excite no
more sensation than his grandmother; and a
newspaper without an elopement, or a breach
of promise, has no news at all.

It is not my desire to affect any singular
exception from established tastes, and I am
ready to confess that the next best thing to
being in love one's self is to speculate on the
hopes and fears and fates of others. Ill tide
the heart that has no sympathy for the little
schemes and subterfuges, which form the only
romance of a world so matter of fact!——I have

never listened to a lame excuse for love's delinquencies without an anxious longing to play the prompter; and have witnessed the ceremony of cross-questioning with as much trepidation as I could have felt had I been the culprit myself. It is not, however, to be maintained that the love adventures of the present age can, in any way, compete with the enchantment of days agone; when tender souls were won by tough exploits, and Cupid's dart was a twenty-foot lance, ordained only to reach the lady's heart through the ribs of the rival. This was the golden age of love, albeit I am not one to lament it, thinking, as I do, that it is far more sensible to aid and abet my neighbour in toasting the beauty of his mistress, than to caper about with him in the lists, for contradiction's sake, to the imminent danger and discomfort of us both. After this came the middle or dark ages of love, when it had ceased to be a glory, but had lost nothing of its fervour as a passion. If there is here less of romance than in the tilting days, there is considerably more of interest, because there is more of mystery. In the one, the test of true love was to make boast ; in the other, it was to keep secret. Accordingly, for an immense space of time, we have nothing but such fragments of adventures as could be gathered by eavesdroppers, who leave us to put head and tail to them as best suits our fancy ; and the loves of Queen Elizabeth, who lived, as it were, only yesterday, are less known than the loves of Queen Genevra, who perhaps never lived at all.

These reflections occurred to me some little time ago, during a twilight reverie in the long, gloomy banqueting-room of Holyrood.   It was the very land of love and mystery, for there was scarcely one of the grim warriors who frowned from the walls but had obtained his share of celebrity in lady's bower, as well as in tented field, and scarcely one of whom the adventures handed down have been more than sufficient to excite curiosity. I continued speculating through this line of kings, blessing the mark and confounding the painter, who has given us so little of their history in their faces, till I grew quite warm upon the subject, and found myself uniting and reasoning upon the few facts of

which we are in possession, till I fancied I
could penetrate through two or three centuries
at least, and supply much of the material in
which history is deficient.

Scotland has, I think, in spite of its sober,
money-making character, always excited a
more romantic curiosity than England. This,
perhaps, is more owing to its peculiar misfortunes than to any particular difference of disposition. Our own heroes have been as brave,
and, no doubt, as loving, but they do not walk
under such a halo of pity; and whilst we pry
with eagerness into the secrets of the gallant
James's, we suffer those of their English con-
temporaries to be "interred with their bones."
I have always felt this strongly, and, at the
time of which I speak, I felt it stronger than
ever. I was treading upon the very boards
which had bounded to their manly steps, and
was surrounded by the very walls which possessed the secret whisperings of their hearts.
From that identical window, perhaps, had the
first James gazed upon the moon, which I saw
rising, and fancied that he almost held com-
mune with the eyes of his English beauty.

There, perhaps, had the royal poet entwined her name with the choicest hopes of his bosom, and woven out a tale of happiness which concealed but too securely the assassin and the dagger behind it. There, too, might the courteous and courageous victims of Flodden Field and Solway Moss have planned the loves which characterised their lives, and the wars which concluded them, almost at the same moment. And there might the hapless Mary have first listened to the poisonous passion of a Darnley, or a Bothwell, and afterwards shed the tears of bitterness and self-reproach.

I paced this sad-looking room of rejoicing quite unconscious of the hours that were passing ; for I was alone, and in a train of thought which nothing but a hearty shake could have interrupted. Mary, and all her beauty and talents and acquirements, continued floating before me. Her world of lovers and admirers, who, for the most part, were sleeping in a bloody bed, seemed rising one by one to my view, and I wandered with them through their hopes, and their fears, and their sorrows, even to the scaffold, as though I had been the

ghost of one of them myself, and were possessed of secrets of which there is no living
record.

Many of these ill-fated hearts have, by their
nobility or their exploits, or by the caprice of
historians, received their full meed of applause
and pity; many, no doubt, have sunk into
oblivion; and some, in addition to their misfortunes, have left their memories to combat
with the censure which has been thought due
to their presumption; — of these last, I have
always considered the unfortunate Chatelar to
have been the most hardly used, and in the
course of my musings I endeavoured to puzzle
out something satisfactory to myself upon his
dark and tragic story.

The birth of Chatelar, if not noble, was in
no common degree honourable, for he was
great-nephew to the celebrated Bayard, *le Che-
valier sans peur et sans reproche.* It is said that
he likewise bore a strong resemblance to him
in person, possessing a handsome face and
graceful figure; and equally in manly and
elegant acquirements, being an expert soldier
and an accomplished courtier. In addition to

this, says Brantome, who knew him person-
ally, he possessed a most refined mind, and
spoke and wrote, both in prose and poetry, as
well as any man in France.

Dangerous indeed are these advantages ; and
Chatelar's first meeting with Mary was under
circumstances calculated to render them doubly
dangerous. Alone, as she conceived herself,
cast off from the dearest ties of her heart, the
land which she had learned to consider her
native land fading fast from her eyes, and the
billows bearing her to the banishment of one
with which, as it contained none that she loved,
she could feel no sympathy ; in this scene of
wailing and tears, the first tones of the poet
were stealing upon her ear with the spirit of
kindred feelings and kindred pursuits. We are
to consider that Mary at this time had obtained but little experience, and was, probably,
not overstocked with prudence ; having scarcely
attained the age of nineteen years. Not only,
are we told, did she listen with complacency
and pleasure to Chatelar's warm and romantic
praises of her beauty, but employed her poetic
talent in approving and replying to them;

putting herself upon a level with her gifted companion, which was morally certain to convert his veneration into feelings more nearly allied to his nature. Had he not been blamed for his presumption, it is probable that he would have been condemned for his stoicism; and his luckless passion is by no means a singular proof that where hearts are cast in kindred moulds it is difficult to recognize extrinsic disparities. Chatelar saw the woman, and forgot the queen; Mary felt the satisfaction, and was blind to the consequences.

It is much to be lamented by the lovers of truth that none of the poetical pieces which are said to have passed between Mary and Chatelar have been handed down to us. One song would have been a more valuable document in the elucidation of their history than all the annals we possess, and would have taught us, at once, the degree of encouragement and intimacy which was permitted. Whatever it was, it was such as to rivet the chains to which a chivalrous character could offer no resistance; and, from the period of their first meeting, we may consider Chatelar the most enthusiastic of Mary's lovers.

How long he continued the admiration and the favourite of Holyrood does not, I believe, appear. It could not, however, have been any considerable time ere he was compelled to return with his friend and patron, Damville, to France, with full reason to lament his voyage to Scotland, and with, probably, a firm determination to revisit it whenever opportunity should permit. This opportunity his evil stars were not long in bringing about. The projected war of faith between Damville's party and the Huguenots afforded him a fair pretext for soliciting a dispensation of his services. Of the first he was a servant, of the last he was a disciple. It was therefore contrary to his honour and inclinations to fight against either of them, and, accordingly, in about fifteen months, we find him again at Holyrood.

Mary, it may reasonably be inferred, from her extreme love of France and unwillingness to leave it, was not very speedily to be reconciled to her change of scene and society; a face, therefore, from the adopted land of her affections, and a tongue capable of gratifying them with the minutest accounts of the beloved objects it contained, must, at this time, have been acquisitions of no small interest; Chatelar, too, had already worked a welcome on his own account.

Few of my readers need be reminded how insensibly and certainly the tongue which speaks of that which is dear to our hearts is stored up with it in the same treasury. The tale and the teller of it—the leaf and the wave it falls upon —arrive at the same time at the same destination. Histories, for the most part, insinuate that Mary's carriage towards Chatelar was merely that of kindness and courtesy; but this, I think, is an inference not warranted by the various facts which they have been unable to repress, and not even the silence of the inveterate John Knox upon this head can convince me that Chatelar had not reason to believe himself beloved.

Let us then imagine, if we can, what was likely to be the intoxication produced in the brain as well as the bosom of a man of an enthusiastic disposition by a free and daily intercourse, during three months, with the fascinations of a creature like Mary. What tales could that old misshapen boudoir, famous only, in common estimation, for the murder of Rizzio and the boot of Darnley, tell of smiles and tears over the fortunes of dear and distant companions of childhood, as narrated by the voice of one to whom, perhaps, they were equally dear! What tales could it tell of mingling music, and mingling poetry, and mingling looks, and vain regrets, and fearful anticipations! Here had the day been passed in listening to the praises of each other, from lips which had made praise their sweetest study; and here had the twilight stolen upon them when none were by, and none could know how deep the fountain from whence those praises proceeded. Let us imagine all this, and, likewise, how Chatelar was likely to be wrought upon by the utter hopelessness of his case.

Had the object of his passion been upon any thing like a level with him, had there been the most remote possibility of its attainment, his subsequent conduct would, most likely, not have been such as to render him a subject for investigation. But Mary must have been as inaccessible to him as the being of another world. The devotion which he felt for her was looked upon by the heads of her Court as a species of sacrilege; and he was given to believe that each had a plan for undermining his happiness and removing him from her favour. If this could not be effected, it was a moral certainty that Mary, in the bloom of her youth and the plenitude of her power, must become to some one of her numerous suitors all which it was impossible that she could ever become to him. Of these two cases, perhaps, the one was as bad as the other, and Chatelar was impelled to an act of desperation which, in these days, can scarcely be conceived. On the night of the 12th of February, 1563, he was found concealed in the young Queen's bed-chamber.

It would, I fear, be a difficult undertaking, in the eyes of dispassionate and reasoning persons, to throw a charitable doubt upon the motives of this unseasonable intrusion. The fair and obvious inference is, that he depended upon the impression he had made upon Mary's heart, and the impossibility of their lawful union. In some degree, too, he might have been influenced by the perilous consequences of a discovery, to which he possibly thought her love would not permit her to expose him. The propriety of this argument, if he made use of it, was not put to the test, for his discovery fell to the lot of Mary's female attendants before she retired.

There is, however, another class of readers who will give him credit for other thoughts. I mean those best of all possible judges of love affairs, in whom the common-places of life have not entirely destroyed that kindly feeling of romance which nature thought it necessary to implant in them, and of which the practice of modern days renders it necessary for them to be ashamed. The readers of whom I speak will decide more from the heart than the head; and then what an interminable field of defence is laid open ! What strange feelings and un-accountable exploits might be furnished from the catalogue of love's vagaries ! Were Chate-lar to be judged by other examples, and in connection with the devoted character of the period, it might not be difficult to believe his conduct as free from evil intention as it was rash and unfortunate. If we keep in mind his poetical temperament and the fantastic lengths to which it was carried in his native country, where ladies' chambers were, and continue to be, very common scenes for the reception of company, his intrusion will, at all events, bear a much fairer interpretation than could be bestowed upon a similar one, under the usages of the society in which we live.

On the following morning, the affair was made known to the Queen by her ladies. Had they been wise enough to hold their peace, it is odds but the lover's taste for adventure would have been satisfied by the first essay. Instead of this, being forbidden all future access to her presence, he became more desperate than ever. His motives had been misconstrued; his actions, he thought, had been misrepresented; he was bent on explanation, and he hoped for pardon. Thus it was that when Mary, on the same day, quitted Edinburgh, her disgraced admirer executed his determination of following her, and, on the night of the 14th, seized the only opportunity of an interview by committing the very same offence for which he was then suffering :——Mary had no sooner entered her chamber than Chatelar stood before her.

Whatever her feelings may have been towards him, it is not surprising that this sudden
apparition should have proved somewhat startling, and have produced an agitation not very
favourable to his cause. It may be presumed
that she was not mistress of her actions, for
certain it is, that she did that which, if she
possessed one half of the womanly tenderness
for which she has credit, must have been a
blight and a bitterness upon her after life.
Chatelar comes, wounded to the quick, to supplicate a hearing; and the Queen, it is said,
"was fain to cry for help," and desire Murray,
who came at her call, "to put his dagger into
him."

Thus, by dint of unnecessary terrors and un-
meaning words, was Chatelar given over to an
enemy who had always kept a jealous eye upon
him, and to justice, which seemed determined
to strain a point for his sake, and give him
something more than his due. In a few days
he was tried, and experienced the usual fate of
favourites, by being condemned to death.

Alas, how bitter is the recollection of even
trifling injuries towards those who loved and

are lost to us ! yet what had this been in coun-
terpoise to the reflections of Mary ?   She had
given over a fond and a fervent heart to death
for no fault but too much love, and any attempt
to recall the deed might have afforded a colour
to the aspersions which malignant persons
were ever ready to cast upon her character, but
could have availed no further.

For Chatelar there was little leisure for reflection.   The fever of the first surprise—the
strange, the appalling conviction as to the hand
which hurled him to his fate—the shame, the
humiliation, the indignation, had scarce time
to cool in his forfeit blood, before he was
brought out to die the death of a culprit upon
the scaffold.

It has been the fashion for writers upon this
subject, in the quiet and safety of their fire-
sides, to exclaim against his want of preparation for his transit; but, under such circumstances, I cannot much wonder that he should
rather rebel against the usual ceremonies of
psalm-singing and last speeches.   If he might
have died more like a priest, it is certain that
he could not have died more like a gallant ca-

valier; and if he chose to nerve himself for death by reading Ronsard's hymn upon it, this is no proof that he looked with irreverence upon what was to follow it. His last words are extremely touching; for they prove that, though he considered that Mary had remorselessly sacrificed his life, his sorrow was greater than his resentment, and his love went with him to the grave. "Adieu," he said, turning to the quarter in which he supposed her to be, "adieu, most beautiful and most cruel princess in the world!" and then, submitting himself to the executioner, he met the last stroke with a courage consistent with his character.

Of Mary's behaviour on this event, history, I believe, gives no account.

My ponderings upon this singular story had detained me long. The old pictures on the walls glistened and glimmered in the moonshine like a band of spectres; and, at last, I fairly fancied that I saw one grisly gentleman pointing at me with his truncheon, in the act of directing his furies to "seize on me and take me to their torments." It was almost time to be gone; but the thought of Chatelar seemed holding me by the skirts. I could not depart without taking another look at the scene of his happiest hours, and I stole, shadow-like, with as little noise as I could, through the narrow passages and staircases, till I stood in Mary's little private apartment.

As I passed the antechamber the light was shining only on the stain of blood; the black shadows here and elsewhere made the walls appear as though they had been hung with mourning; and the ghost of a tune was haunting my ears with—"*Adieu plaisant pays de France.*" I do not know that ever I felt so melancholy; and had not the owl just then given a most dismal whoop, I think I might very possibly have had courage and sentiment enough to remain till I was safely locked up for the night. I passed by the low bed, under which Chatelar is said to have hidden himself. It must have cost him some trouble to get there! I glanced hastily at the faded tambour work, which, it is possible, he might have witnessed in its progress; and I shook my head with much satisfaction to think that I had a head to shake. "If," said I,

" there is more interest attached to the old times of love, it is, after all, in some degree, counterbalanced by the safety of the present; and I know not whether it is not better to be born in the age when racks and torments are used metaphorically, than in those in which it is an even chance that I might have encountered the reality."

LADY BETTY'S POCKET-BOOK.

"Into it, Knight, thou must not look."

Scott.

I PASSED my five-and-twentieth birthday at Oakenshade. Sweet sentimental age! Dear, deeply regretted place! Oakenshade is the fairest child of Father Thames, from Gloucestershire to Blackwall. She is the very queen of cottages, for she has fourteen best bedrooms and stabling for a squadron. Her trees are the finest in Europe, and her inhabitants the fairest in the world. Her old mistress is the Lady Bountiful of the country, and her young mistresses are the prides of it. Lady Barbara is black-eyed and hyacinthine, Lady Betty blue-eyed and Madonna-wised.

In situations of this kind it is absolutely necessary for a man to fall in love, and, in due compliance with established customs, I fell in love both with Lady Betty and Lady Barbara. Now Barbara was soft-hearted and high-minded, and pretended, as I thought, not to care for me, that she might not interfere with the interests of her sister; and Betty was reckless and giddy-witted, and troubled her head about nobody and nothing upon earth, except the delightful occupation of doing what she pleased. Accordingly, we became the Romeo and Juliet of the place, excepting that I never could sigh, and she never could apostrophize.

Oh, what a time was that! I will just give a sample of a day. We rose at seven (it was July), and wandered amongst moss roses, velvet lawns, and sequestered summer-houses, till the lady mother summoned us to the breakfast table. I know not how it was, but the footman on these occasions always found dear Barbara absent on a butterfly chase, gathering flowers, or feeding her pet robin, and Betty and myself on a sweet honeysuckle seat, just big enough to hold two, and hidden round a happy corner as snug as a bird's nest. The moment the villain came within hearing, I used to begin in an audible voice to discourse upon the beauties of nature, and Betty would answer in the same key, as if the subject were the nearest to her heart.

After breakfast we used to retire to the young ladies' study, in which blest retreat I filled some hundred pages of their albums, whilst Betty looked over my shoulder, and Barbara hammered with all her might upon the grand piano, that we might not be afraid to talk. I was acknowledged to be the prince of poets and riddle-mongers, and, in the graphic art, I was a prodigy unrivalled. *Sans doute*, I was a little overrated. My riddles were so plain, and my metaphors so puzzling — and then my trees were like mountains, and my men were like monkeys. But love has such penetrating optics ! Lady Betty could perceive beauties to which the rest of the world were perfectly blind, and, for hours together, I have felt her pretty lips exhaling their perfumes within a quarter of an inch of my temples. It was a perilous situation. It used to take away my breath — even Betty's was drawn shorter, and she would hail Barbara through the thunders of Kalkbrenner, as much as to say that things were in a dangerous state, and it was time to take a ride.

Now Barbara was a good horsewoman, and Betty was a bad one; consequently, Barbara rode a pony, and Betty rode a donkey; consequently, Barbara rode a mile before, and Betty rode a mile behind; and, consequently, it was absolutely necessary for me to keep fast hold of Betty's hand, for fear she should tumble off. Thus did we journey through wood and through valley, through the loveliest and most love-making scenes that ever figured in rhyme or on canvass. The trees never looked so green, the flowers never smelt so sweet, and the exercise and the fears of her high-mettled palfrey gave my companion a blush which is quite beyond the reach of simile. Of course, we always lost ourselves, and trusted to Barbara to guide us home, which she generally did by the most circuitous routes she could find.

At dinner, the lady-mother would inquire

where we had been, but none of us could tell excepting Barbara. "Why, Betty, my dear, you understood our geography well enough when you were guide to our good old friend the General!" Ah, but Betty found it was quite a different thing to be guide to her good young friend the captain; and her explanation was generally a zigzag sort of performance, which outdid the best riddle in her album.

It was the custom of the lady-mother to take a nap after dinner, and, having a due regard for her, we always left her to this enjoyment as soon as possible. Sometimes we floated in a little skiff down the broad and tranquil river, which, kindled by the setting sun, moved onward like a stream of fire, tuning our voices to glees and duetts, till the nightingales themselves were astonished. Oh, the witchery of bright eyes at sunset and music on the water! Sometimes we stole through the cavernous recesses of the old oak wood, conjuring up fawns and satyrs at every step, and sending Barbara to detect the deceptions, and play at hide and seek with us. At last our mistress, the moon, would open her eye and warn us home, where, on the little study sofa, we watched her progress, repeated sweet poesy, and told ghost stories till we frightened ourselves under one another's wings like chickens in a storm.   Many a time did I long to break the footman's head when he brought the lights and announced the tea.   The lady-mother never slept after this, and the business of the day was ended.

Things went on in this way for a week or ten days, and Lady Betty appeared to have less spirits, and a more serious and languid air than heretofore.   There was now nothing hoydenish in her behaviour, and, instead of the upper lip curling with scorn, the under one was drooping with sentiment.   Her voice was not so loud, and fell in a gentler cadence, and the Madonna braid was festooned with a more exquisite grace.   When I besought her to let me hear the subject of her thoughts, the little budget was always of such a mournful description, that I could not choose but use my tenderest mode of comforting.   She had, she knew not why, become more serious.   She supposed it was because she was growing older—she hoped it was because she was growing better. In fine, she had determined to amend her life, and appointed me master of the ceremonies to her conscience, which, sooth to say, had been in a woful state of misrule.

I could not, of course, have any doubt that my sweet society had been the cause of this metamorphosis, and I congratulated myself fervently. She was becoming the very pattern for a wife, and I contemplated in her the partner of my declining years, the soother of my cares, the mother of my precious babes. It was cruel to postpone my declaration, but I was always a little given to caution. Lady Betty had been a sad madcap, and might not this be a mere freak of the moment? Besides, there was a charm about our little forbidden endearments, of which a declared and licensed lover has no idea, so I determined to observe and act with deliberation.

Our pastimes continued the same as before, and our interchanges of kindness increased. Amongst other things, Lady Betty signalized me by a purse and a pencil-case, and in return was troubled with an extreme longing for a lilac and gold pocket-book, in which I was sometimes rash enough to note down my fugitive thoughts. It had been given me by——no matter whom——there was nothing on earth that I would not have sacrificed to Lady Betty. She received it in both her hands, pressed it to her bosom, and promised faithfully that she would pursue the plan I had adopted in it; casting up her delinquencies at the end of the year, with a serious view to amendment.

Alas! the pinnacle of happiness is but a sorry resting place, from which the chief occupation of mankind is to push one another headlong! Of my own case I have particular reason to complain, for I was precipitated from the midst of my burning, palpitating existence, by the veriest blockhead in life. He came upon us like the Simoom, devastating every green spot in his progress, and leaving our hearts a blank. In short, he was a spark of quality, who drove four bloods, and cut his own coats. His visage was dangerously dissipated and cadaverous, his figure as taper as a fishing-rod, and his manner had a *je ne sais quoi* of languid impertinence, which was a great deal too over-whelming. Altogether, he was a gallant whose incursion would have caused me very consider-able uneasiness, had I not felt secure that my mistress was already won.

I shall never forget the bustle which was oc-casioned by the arrival of this worthy. He was some sort of connexion to the lady-mother, thought himself privileged to come without in-vitation, and declared his intention of remain-ing till he was tired. He ordered the servants about, and gave directions for his accommoda-tion precisely as if he had been at home, and scarcely deigned to tender his forefinger to the ladies till he had made himself perfectly com-fortable. When I was introduced from the back-ground, from which I had been scowling with indignation and amazement, he regarded my common-place appearance with careless contempt, made me a bow as cold as if it had come from Lapland, and, in return, received one from the North Pole. I considered that he was usurping all my rights in the establish-ment; his freedoms with Betty and Barbara were a violation of my private property, and I even grudged him his jokes with the lady-mother. We were foes from first sight.

Lady Betty saw how the spirit was working within me, and hastened to prevent its effervescence. She gave me one of her overpowering looks, and besought me to assist her in being civil to him, for, in truth, the attentions of common politeness had already completely exhausted her. I was quite charmed with the vexation she felt at his intrusion, and loved her a thousand times better because she detested him. His visit, indeed, had such an effect upon her, that, before the day was over, she complained to me, in confidence, of being seriously unwell.

From this time, the whole tenor of our amusements was revolutionized. Lady Betty's illness was not fancied; she was too weak to ride her donkey, too qualmish to go inside the barouche, which was turned out every day to keep the bloods in wind, and nothing agreed with her delicate health but being mounted on the box beside Lord S———. The evenings passed off as heavily as the mornings. Lady

Barbara used to ask me to take the usual stroll with her, and Lady Betty, being afraid to venture upon the damp grass, was again left to the mercy of Lord S——, to whom walking was a low-lifed amusement, for which he had no taste. The lady-mother, as usual, had her sleeping fits, and, when we returned, we invariably found things topsy-turvy, and totally out of order. The candles had not been lighted, the tea-things had not been laid, and Lord S—— had turned sulky with his bottle, and was sitting in the dark with Lady Betty. I felt for her more than I can express, and could not, for the life of me, conceive where she picked up patience to be civil to him. She even affected to be delighted with his conversation, and her good-breeding was beyond all praise.

With such an example of endurance before me, and the pacific promises which I had made, I could not avoid carrying a benevolent aspect. Indeed, though the enemy had effectually cut off the direct communication of sentiment between us, I was not altogether without my triumphs and secret satisfactions. The general outline which I have given was occasionally intersected with little episodes which were quite charming. For instance, Lady Betty used constantly to employ me upon errands to her mother, who was usually absent in her private room, manufacturing caudle and flannel petticoats for the work-house. When I returned, she would despatch me to her sister, who was requiring my advice upon her drawing, in the study ; and thus Lord S—— could not fail to observe our familiar terms, and that we perfectly understood each other. What gave me more pleasure than all was, that he must see I had no fears of leaving my liege lady alone with him, which must have galled him to the quick. When she had no other means of showing her devotion to me, she would produce the lilac pocket-book, and pursue the work of amendment which I had suggested to her ; indeed, this was done with a regularity which, when I considered her former hair-brained character, I knew could only be sustained by the most ardent attachment.——My pride and my passion increased daily.

At last, by a happy reverse of fortune, I was

led to look for the termination of my trials. Lord S—— was a personage of too great importance to the nation to be permitted to enjoy his own peace and quiet, and his bilious visage was required to countenance mighty concerns in other parts. His dressing-case was packed up, and the barouche was ordered to the door, but poor Lady Betty was still doomed to be a sufferer; she was, somehow or other, hampered with an engagement to ride with him as far as the village, in order to pay a visit for her mother to the charity-school, and I saw her borne off, the most bewitching example of patience and resignation. I did not offer to accompany them, for I thought it would have looked like jealousy, but engaged, in answer to a sweetly whispered invitation, to meet her in her walk back.

When I returned to the drawing-room, Barbara and the lady-mother were absent on their usual occupations, and I sat down for a moment of happy reflection on the delights which awaited me. My heart was tingling with anticipation, and every thought was poetry. A scrap

of paper lay upon the table, and was presently
enriched with a sonnet on each side, which I
had the vanity to think were quite good enough
to be transferred to Lady Betty's most beloved
and lilac pocket-book.   I raised my eyes, and,
lo ! in the bustle of parting with Lord S——,
she had forgotten to deposit it in her desk.
What an agreeable surprise it would be for her
to find how I had been employed ! How fondly
would she thank me for such a delicate mode
of showing my attention !   The sonnets were
written in my best hand, and I was about to
close the book, when I was struck with the extreme beauty of Lady Betty's.   Might I venture to peruse a page or so, and enjoy the
luxury of knowing her private thoughts of me ?
Nay, was it not evidently a sweet little finesse
to teach me the secrets of her heart, and should
I not mortify her exceedingly if I neglected to
take advantage of it ? This reflection was quite
sufficient, and I commenced the chronicle of
her innocent cogitations forthwith.   It began
with noting the day of the month on which I
had presented the gift, and stated, prettily,
the plan of improvement which I had sug-

gested.   The very first memorandum contained
her reasons for loving her dear M——.   I
pressed the book to my lips, and proceeded
to

" REASON THE FIRST.

" A good temper is better in a companion
than a great wit.   If dear M—— is deficient in the latter, it is not his fault, and
his excellence in the former makes ample
amends."

How! As much as to say I am a good-natured
fool.   Was there no other construction ?   No
error of the press ?   None.   The context assured me that I was not mistaken.

" REASON THE SECOND.

" Personal beauty is not requisite in a husband, and if he is a little mistaken in his estimate of himself in this respect, it will make
him happy, and save me the trouble of labouring for that end."

Conceited and ill-favoured ! My head began
to swim.

" REASON THE THIRD.

" I have been told that very passionate at-
tachments between married people are produc-

tive of much disquietude and jealousy. The temperate regard, therefore, which I feel for dear M—— argues well for the serenity of our lives—Heigh-ho!"

Furies!

" REASON THE FOURTH.

" I have sometimes doubted whether this temperate regard be really love, but, as pity is next a-kin to love, and I pity him on so many points, I think I cannot be mistaken."

Pity!

" REASON THE FIFTH.

" I pity him because it is necessary that I should place him on the shelf during Lord S—'s visit, for fear S— should be discouraged by appearances, and not make the declaration which I have been so long expecting."

Place me on the shelf!!

" REASON THE SIXTH.

" I pity him, because, if S— really comes forward, I shall be obliged to submit poor dear M— to the mortification of a dismissal."

!!!

" REASON THE SEVENTH.

" I pity him, because he is so extremely

kind and obliging in quitting the room whenever his presence becomes troublesome."

! ! ! !

" REASON THE EIGHTH.

"I pity him, because his great confidence in my affection makes him appear so ridiculous, and because S— laughs at him."

! ! ! ! !

"REASON THE NINTH.

"I pity him, because, if I do ultimately marry him, S— will tell every body that it is only because I could not obtain the barouche and four—Heigh—heigh ho!"

! ! ! ! ! !

"REASON THE TENTH.

"I pity him, because he has so kindly consented to meet me on my return from the charity-school, without once suspecting that I go to give S— a last opportunity. He is really a very good young man—Ah, well-a-day!"—

And ah, well-a-day ! ! ! ! ! ! &c., &c.—Let no man, henceforth, endeavour to enjoy the luxury of his mistress' secret thoughts.

I closed the book, and walked to the window. The river flowed temptingly beneath it.

Would it be best to drown myself or shoot myself? Or would it be best to take horse after the barouche, and shoot Lord S——? I was puzzled with the alternatives. It was absolutely necessary that *somebody* should be put to death, but my confusion was too great to decide upon the victim.

At this critical juncture of my fate, when I was wavering between the gallows and "a grave where four roads meet," Lady Barbara came dancing in, to request my assistance upon her drawing. She was petrified at my suicidal appearance, and, indeed, seemed in doubt whether the act of immolation had not been already effected. Her fears rushed in crimson to her cheek, as she inquired the cause of my disorder; and her beauty and the interesting concern she expressed cast an entire new light upon me. I would be revenged on Lady Betty in a manner far more cutting than either drowning or shooting. Barbara was the prettiest by far—Barbara was the best by infinity. Sweet, simple, gentle Barbara! How generously had she sacrificed her feelings, and given me up to her sister! How happy was I to have it in my power to reward her for it ! *She* now should be the partner of my declining years, the soother of my cares, the mother of my precious babes ; and as for Lady Betty—I renounced her. I found that my heart had all along been Barbara's, and I congratulated myself upon being brought to my senses.

The business was soon opened, and we were all eloquence and blushes. I expressed my warm admiration of her self-denial and affection for her sister ; hinted at my knowledge of her sentiments for myself; explained every particular of my passion, prospects, and genealogy, fixed upon our place of residence, and allotted her pin-money. It was now Barbara's turn. " She was confused—she was distressed —she feared—she hoped—she knew not what to say." She paused for composure, and I waited in an ecstasy—" Why," I exclaimed, " why will you hesitate, my own, my gentle Barbara ? Let me not lose one delicious word of this heavenly confession." Barbara regained her courage. " Indeed, then—indeed, and indeed—I have been engaged to my cousin for more than three years !"

This was a stroke upon which I had never once calculated, and my astonishment was awful. Barbara then was not in love with me after all, and the concern which I had felt for her blighted affections was altogether erroneous ! I had made the proposal to be revenged on Lady Betty, and my disappointment had completely turned the tables upon me. Instead of bringing her to shame, I was ashamed of myself, and my mortification made me feel as though she had heaped a new injury upon me. What I said upon the occasion I cannot precisely remember, and if I could, I doubt whether my reader would be able to make head or tail of it. I concluded, however, with my compliments to the lady-mother, and an urgent necessity to decamp. Barbara knew not whether she ought to laugh or to cry. I gave her no time to recover herself, for Betty would be home presently, and it was material to be off before they had an opportunity of comparing notes. In three minutes I was mounted on my horse, and again ruminating on the various advantages of hanging, drowning, and shooting.

I thought I had got clear off, but at the end
of the lawn I was fated to encounter the bewitching smile of Lady Betty on her return
from the village.   Her words were brimming
with tenderness, and her delight to be rid of
that odious Lord S—— was beyond measure.
It had quite restored her to health, she was
able to recommence her rides, and would
order the donkey to be got ready immediately.

So, then, it appeared that the drive to the
charity-school had not answered the purpose
after all, and I was to be the *locum tenens* of
Lady Betty's affections till the arrival of a new
acquaintance.   I know not whether my constitution is different from that of other people.
A pretty face is certainly a terrible criterion of
a man's resolution ; but, for the honour of man-
hood, I contrived for once to be superior to its
fascinations.   To adhere strictly to truth, I
must confess, however humiliating the confession may be, that this dignified behaviour
was very materially sustained by the transactions with Lady Barbara, for the consequence
of whose communications there was no answer-
ing.   I declined the donkey ride, looked a most

explanatory look of reproach, and declared my necessity of returning to town. Lady Betty was amazed — remonstrated — intreated — looked like an angel—and finally put her handkerchief to her eyes.

There was no standing this. "I go," said I, "I go, because it is proper to quit whenever my *presence becomes troublesome*—I will not oblige you to *put me on the shelf*—I will not be too encroaching upon your *temperate regard — Heigh — heigh-ho !*" With that I plunged the spurs into my steed, and vanished at full gallop.

It was long before I heard anything more of Oakenshade or its inhabitants. In the middle of the following December I received a piece of wedding-cake from the gentle Barbara, and in the same packet a letter from Lady Betty.

She had written instead of mamma, who was troubled with a gouty affection in the hand. She spoke much (and I have no doubt sincerely) of the cruel separation from her sister. Touched feelingly upon the happiness of the time I had spent at Oakenshade, and trusted she might venture to claim a week of me at Christmas. She was truly sorry that she had no inducement to hold out beyond the satisfaction of communicating happiness, which she knew was always a paramount feeling with me. She was all alone, and wretched in the long evenings when mamma went to sleep; and reverted plaintively and prettily to the little study and the ghost stories. As for the lilac pocket-book, she had cast up her follies and misdemeanors, and found the total, even *before* the end of the year, so brimfull of shame and repentance, that she had indignantly thrown it into the fire, trusting to my kindness to give her another with fresh advice.

Dear Lady Betty! my resentment was long gone by—I had long felt a conviction that her little follies were blameless, and not at all uncommon; and I vow that had her happiness depended upon me, I would have done anything to ensure it. I was obliged, however, to send an excuse for the present, for I had only been married a week.

INSURANCE AND ASSURANCE.

Bernardine.—I have been drinking hard all night, and will have more time to prepare me, or they shall beat out my brains with billets. I will not consent to die this day, that's certain.

Duke.—Oh, Sir, you must; and therefore I beseech you look forward on the journey you shall go.

Bernardine.—I swear I will not die to-day for any man's persuasion.

Measure for Measure.

" IT is inconceivable to the virtuous and praiseworthy part of the world, who have been born and bred to respectable idleness, what terrible straits are the lot of those scandalous rogues whom Fortune has left to shift for themselves!"

Such was my feeling ejaculation when, full of penitence for the sin of urgent necessity, I wended my way to the attorney who had swept together, and, for the most part, pecked up, the crumbs which fell from my father's table.   He was a little, grizzled, sardonic animal, with features which were as hard as his heart, and fitted their leather-jacket so tightly that one would have thought it had shrunk from washing, or that they had bought it second-hand and were pretty nearly out at the elbows. They were completely emblematic of their possessor, whose religion it was to make the most of every thing, and, amongst the rest, of the distresses of his particular friends, amongst whom I had the happiness of standing very forward.   My business required but little explanation, for I was oppressed by neither rent-rolls nor title-deeds; and we sat down to consider the readiest means of turning an excellent income for one year into something decent for a few more.

My adviser, whose small, experienced eye had twinkled through all the speculations of the age, and, at the same time, had taken a very exact admeasurement of my capabilities of turning them to advantage, seemed to be of opinion that I was fit for nothing on earth.

For one undertaking I wanted application; for another I wanted capital. "Now," said he, " as the first of these deficiencies is irremediable, we must do what we can to supply the latter. Take my advice—Insure your life for a few thousands ; you will have but little premium to pay, for you look as if you would live for ever; and from my knowledge of your rattle-pated habits and the various chances against you, I will give you a handsome sum for the insurance."

Necessity obliged me to acquiesce in the proposal, and I assured the old cormorant that there was every likelihood of my requiting his liberality by the most unremitting perseverance in all the evil habits which had procured me his countenance. We shook hands in mutual ill-opinion, and he obligingly volunteered to accompany me to an Insurance Office, where they were supposed to estimate the duration of a man's life to a quarter of an hour and odd seconds.

We arrived a little before the business hour, and were shown into a large room, where we found several more speculators waiting ruefully for the oracle to pronounce sentence. In the centre was a large table, round which, at equal distances, were placed certain little lumps of money, which my friend told me were to reward the labours of the Inquisition, amongst whom the surplus arising from absentees would likewise be divided. From the keenness with which each individual darted upon his share and ogled that of his absent neighbour, I surmised that some of my fellow-sufferers would find the day against them. They would be examined by eyes capable of penetrating every crevice of their constitutions, by noses which could smell a rat a mile off, and hunt a guinea breast high. How indeed could plague or pestilence, gout or gluttony, expect to lurk in its hole undisturbed when surrounded by a pack of terriers which seemed hungry enough to devour one another? Whenever the door slammed, and they looked for an addition to their cry, they seemed for all the world as though they were going to bark; and if a straggler really entered and seized upon his portion the intelligent look of vexation was precisely like that of a dog who has lost a bone. When ten or a dozen of these gentry had assembled, the labours of the day commenced.

Most of our adventurers for raising supplies upon their natural lives were afflicted with a natural conceit that they were by no means circumscribed in foundation for such a project. In vain did the Board endeavour to persuade them that they were half dead already. They fought hard for a few more years, swore that their fathers had been almost immortal, and that their whole families had been as tenacious of life as so many eels. Alas! they were first ordered into an adjoining room, which I soon learnt was the condemned cell, and then delicately informed that the establishment could have nothing to say to them. Some indeed had the good luck to be reprieved a little longer, but even these did not effect a very flattering or advantageous bargain. One old gentleman had a large premium to pay for a totter in his knees; another for an extraordinary circumference in the girth; and a dowager of high respectability, who was afflicted with certain undue proportions of width, was fined most exorbitantly. The only customer who met with any thing like satisfaction was a gigantic man of Ireland, with whom Death, I thought, was likely to have a puzzling contest.

"How old are you, sir?" inquired an exaaminer.

"Forty."

"You seem a strong man?"

"I am the strongest man in Ireland."

"But subject to the gout?"

"No. — The rheumatism. — Nothing else, upon my soul."

"What age was your father when he died?"

"Oh, he died young; but then he was killed in a row."

"Have you any uncles alive?"

"No: they were all killed in rows too."

"Pray, sir, do you think of returning to Ireland?"

"May be I shall, some day or other."

"What security can we have that you are not killed in a row yourself?"

"Oh, never fear! I am the sweetest temper in the world, barring when I'm dining out, which is not often."

" What, sir, you can drink a little ?"

" Three bottles, with ease."

" Ay, that is bad. You have a red face and look apoplectic. You will, no doubt, go off suddenly."

" Devil a bit. My red face was born with me ; and I'll lay a bet I live longer than any two in the room."

" But three bottles ———"

" Never you mind that. I don't mean to drink more than a bottle and a half in future. Besides, I intend to get married, if I can, and live snug."

A debate arose amongst the directors respecting this gentleman's elegibility. The words " row" and " three bottles" ran, hurry-scurry, round the table. Every dog had a snap at them. At last, however, the leader of the pack addressed him in a demurring growl, and agreed that, upon his paying a slight additional premium for his irregularities, he should be admitted as a fit subject.

It was now my turn to exhibit ; but, as my friend was handing me forward, my progress was arrested by the entrance of a young lady with an elderly maid-servant. She was dressed in slight mourning, was the most sparkling beauty I had ever seen, and appeared to produce an instantaneous effect, even upon the stony-hearted directors themselves. The chairman politely requested her to take a seat at the table, and immediately entered into her business, which seemed little more than to show herself and be entitled to twenty thousand pounds, for which her *late husband* had insured his life.

"Zounds," thought I, "twenty thousand pounds and a widow!"

"Ah, Madam," observed the chairman, "your husband made too good a bargain with us. I told him he was an elderly, sickly sort of a man, and not likely to last ; but I never thought he would have died so soon after his marriage."

An elderly, sickly sort of a man ! She would marry again, of course ! I was on fire to be examined before her, and let her hear a favourable report of me. As luck would have it, she had some further transactions, which required certain papers to be sent for, and, in the pause, I stepped boldly forward.

" Gentlemen," said my lawyer, with a smile which whitened the tip of his nose, and very nearly sent it through the external teguments, " allow me to introduce Mr. ———, a particular friend of mine, who is desirous of insuring his life. You perceive he is not one of your dying sort."

The directors turned their eyes towards me with evident satisfaction, and I had the vanity to believe that the widow did so too.

" You have a good broad chest," said one. " I dare say your lungs are never affected."

" Good shoulders too," said another. "Not likely to be knocked down in a row."

" Strong in the legs, and not debilitated by dissipation," cried a third. " I think this gentleman will suit us."

I could perceive that, during these compliments and a few others, the widow was very much inclined to titter, which I considered as much as a flirtation commenced; and when I was ordered into another room to be farther examined by the surgeon in attendance, I longed to tell her to stop till I came back. The professional gentleman did his utmost to

M 5

find a flaw in me, but was obliged to write a certificate, with which I re-entered, and had the satisfaction of hearing the chairman read that I was warranted sound.   The Board congratulated me somewhat jocosely, and the widow laughed outright.   Our affairs were settled exactly at the same moment, and I followed her closely down stairs.

"What mad trick are you at now?" inquired the cormorant.

"I am going to hand that lady to her carriage," I responded; and I kept my word. She bowed to me with much courtesy, laughed again, and desired her servant to drive home.

"Where is that, John?" said I.

"Number ——, sir, in —— street," said John; and away they went.——

We walked steadily along, the bird of prey reckoning up the advantages of his bargain with me, and I in a mood of equally interesting reflection.

"What are you pondering about, young gentleman?" he at last commenced.

"I am pondering whether or no you have not overreached yourself in this transaction."

" How so ? "

" Why I begin to think I shall be obliged to give up my harum-scarum way of life ; drink moderately, leave off fox-hunting, and sell my spirited horses, which, you know, will make a material difference in the probable date of my demise."

" But where is the necessity for your doing all this ? "

" My wife will, most likely, make it a stipulation."

" Your wife ! "

" Yes.   That pretty disconsolate widow we have just parted from.   You may laugh ; but, if you choose to bet the insurance which you have bought of me against the purchase-money, I will take you that she makes me a sedate married man in less than two months."

" Done ! " said cormorant, his features again straining their buck-skins at the idea of having made a double profit of me.   " Let us go to my house, and I will draw a deed to that effect, *gratis*."

I did not flinch from the agreement.   My case, I knew, was desperate.   I should have hanged myself a month before had it not been for the Epsom Races, at which I had particular business; and any little additional reason for disgust to the world would, I thought, be rather a pleasure than a pain—provided I was disappointed in the lovely widow.

Modesty is a sad bugbear upon fortune. I have known many who have not been oppressed by it remain in the shade, but I have never known one who emerged with it into prosperity. In my own case it was by no means a family disease, nor had I lived in any way by which I was likely to contract it. Accordingly, on the following day, I caught myself very coolly knocking at the widow's door; and so entirely had I been occupied in considering the various blessings which would accrue to both of us from our union, that I was half way up stairs before I began to think of an excuse for my intrusion. The drawing-room was vacant, and I was left for a moment to wonder whether I was not actually in some temple of the Loves and Graces. There was not a thing to be seen which did not breathe with tenderness. The ceiling displayed a little heaven of sportive Cupids, the carpet a wilderness of turtle-doves. The pictures were a series of the loves of Jupiter, the vases presented nothing but heartsease and love-lies-bleeding; the very Canary birds were inspired, and had a nest with two young ones; and the cat herself looked kindly over the budding beauties of a tortoise-shell kitten. What a place for a sensitive heart like mine! I could not bear to look upon the mirrors which reflected my broad shoulders on every side, like so many giants; and would have given the world to appear a little pale and interesting, although it might have injured my life a dozen years' purchase.

Nevertheless, I was not daunted, and I looked round, for something to talk about, on the beauty's usual occupations, which I found were all in a tone with what I had before remarked. Upon the open piano lay "Auld Robin Grey," which had, no doubt, been sung in allusion to her late husband. On the table was a half-finished drawing of Apollo, which was, equally without doubt, meant to apply to her future one; and round about were strewed the seductive tomes of Moore, Campbell, and Byron. This witch, thought I, is the very creature I have been sighing after! I would have married her out of a hedge-way, and worked upon the roads to maintain her; but with twenty thousand pounds—ay, and much more, unless I am mistaken, she would create a fever in the frosty Caucasus!

I was in the most melting mood alive, when the door opened, and in walked the fascinating object of my speculations. She was dressed in simple grey, wholly without ornament, and her dark-brown hair was braided demurely over a forehead which looked as lofty as her face was lovely. The reception she gave me was polite and graceful, but somewhat distant; and I perceived that she had either forgotten, or was determined not to recognize, me. I was not quite prepared for this, and, in spite of my constitutional confidence, felt not a little embarrassed. I had, perhaps, mistaken the breakings forth of a young and buoyant spirit, under ridiculous circumstances, for the encouragements of volatile coquetry; and, for a moment, I was in doubt whether I should not apologize and pretend that she was not the lady for whom my visit was intended. But then she was so beautiful! Angels and ministers! Nothing on earth could have sent me down stairs unless I had been kicked down! "Madam," I began —but my blood was in a turmoil, and I have never been able to recollect precisely what I said. Something it was, however, about my late father and her lamented husband, absence and the East Indies, liver complaints and Life Insurance; with compliments, condolences, pardon, perturbation, and preter-plu-perfect impertinence. The lady looked surprised, broke my speech with two or three well-bred ejaculations, and astonished me very much by protesting that she had never heard her husband mention either my father or his promising little heir-apparent, William Henry Thomas, in the whole course of their union.

"Ah, Madam," said I, "the omission is extremely natural! I am sure I am not at all offended with your late husband on that score. He was an elderly, sickly sort of a man. My father always told him he could not last, but he never thought he would have died so

soon after his marriage. He had not time
—he had not time, Madam, to make his
friends happy by introducing them to you."

I believe, upon the whole, I must have behaved remarkably well, for the widow could
not quite make up her mind whether to credit
me or not, which, when we consider the very
slender materials I had to work upon, is saying
a great deal.   At last I contrived to make the
conversation glide away to Auld Robin Grey
and the drawing of Apollo, which I pronounced
to be a *chef-d'œuvre*.   " Permit me, however
to suggest, that the symmetry of the figure
would not be destroyed by a little more of
Hercules in the shoulders, which would make
his life worth a much longer purchase. A little
more amplitude in the chest too, and a trifle
stronger on the legs, as they say at the Insurance Office."

The widow looked comically at the recollections which I had brought to her mind ; her
rosy lips began to disclose their treasures in a
half smile ; and this, in turn, expanded into a
laugh like the laugh of Euphrosyne. This was
the very thing for me.   I was always rather

dashed by beauty on the stilts ; but put us upon fair ground, and I never supposed that I could be otherwise than charming. I ran over all the amusing topics of the day, expended a thousand admirable jokes, repeated touching passages from a new poem which she had not read, laughed, sentimentalized, cuddled the kitten, and forgot to go away till I had sojourned full two hours. Euphrosyne quite lost sight of my questionable introduction, and chimed in with a wit as brilliant as her beauty ; nor did she put on a single grave look when I volunteered to call the next day and read the remainder of the poem.

It is impossible to conceive how carefully I walked home. My head and heart were full of the widow and the wager, and my life was more precious than the Pigot Diamond. I kept my eye sedulously upon the pavement, to be sure that the coal-holes were closed ; and I never once crossed the street without looking both ways,' to calculate the dangers of being run over. When I arrived, I was presented with a letter from my attorney, giving me the choice of an ensigncy in a regiment which was ordered to Sierra Leone, or of going missionary to New Zealand.   I wrote to him, in answer, that it was perfectly immaterial to me whether I was cut off by fever or devoured by cannibals, but that I had business which would prevent me from availing myself of either alternative for two months, at least.

The next morning found me again at the door of Euphrosyne, who gave me her lily hand, and received me with the smile of an old acquaintance.   Affairs went on pretty much the same as they did on the preceding day.   The poem was long, her singing exquisite, my anecdote of New Zealand irresistible, and we again forgot ourselves till it was necessary, in common politeness, to ask me to dinner.   Here her sober attire, which for some months had been a piece of mere gratuitous respect, was exchanged for a low evening dress, and my soul, which was brimming before, was in an agony to find room for my increasing transports. Her spirits were sportive as butterflies, and fluttered over the flowers of her imagination with a grace that was quite miraculous. She ridiculed the rapidity of our acquaintance, eulogized my modesty till it was well nigh burnt to a cinder, and every now and then sharpened her wit by a delicate recurrence to Apollo and the shoulders of Hercules.

The third, and the fourth, and the fifth day, with twice as many more, were equally productive of excuses for calling, and reasons for remaining, till at last I took upon me to call and remain without troubling myself about the one or the other. I was received with progressive cordiality; and, at last, with a mixture of timidity which assured me of the anticipation of a catastrophe which was, at once, to decide the question with the Insurance Office, and determine the course of my travels. One day I found the Peri sitting rather pensively at work, and, as usual, I took my seat opposite to her.

"I have been thinking," said she, "that I have been mightily imposed upon."

"By whom?" I inquired.

"By one of whom you have the highest opinion — by yourself."

"In what do you mistrust me?"

"Come, now, will it please you to be candid, and tell me honestly that all that exceedingly intelligible story about your father, and the liver complaint, and Heaven knows what, was a mere fabrication ? "

" Will it please you to let me thread that needle, for I see that you are taking aim at the wrong end of it ? "

" Nonsense ! Will you answer me ? "

" I think I could put the finishing touch to that sprig.   Do you not see ? "   I continued, jumping up and leaning over her.   " It should be done so—and then so.—What stitch do you call that ? "

The beauty was not altogether in a mood for joking.   I took her hand — it trembled — and so did mine.

" Will you pardon me ? " I whispered.   " I am a sinner, a counterfeit, a poor, swindling disreputable vagabond——but I love you to my soul."

The work dropped upon her knee.

*   *   *   *   *   *   *

In about a fortnight from this time I addressed the following note to my friend.

Dear Sir,

It will give you great pleasure to hear that my prospects are mending, and

that you have lost your wager.   As I intend
settling the insurance on my wife, I shall, of
course, think you entitled to the job.   Should
your trifling loss in me oblige you to become
an ensign to Sierra Leone, or a missionary
to New Zealand, you may rely upon my interest
there.

THE ALBUM.

This is
The patroness of heavenly harmony.
Taming of the Shrew.

IN this age of reviews, when every author who puts forth his book, and every painter who exhibits his picture, is sure of the gratification of reading his character wherever he goes, it appears peculiarly hard that a very important description of work, which unites the beauties of them both, should be altogether neglected. I mean those excellent establishments for the encouragement of literature and the fine arts called Ladies' Albums, the rapid increase of which has done such visible wonders for the benefit of polite society. How many of the choice geniuses of the age are here indebted for their first inspiration!—How many, but for this, had been compelled to remain on their perch for want of a fair field to try their wings, and how greedily will posterity scramble after gilt-edged books with golden clasps to trace the germ of the great works which have descended to them! Alas! had our grandmothers — but it cannot be helped, and every happy undertaking like the invention of Albums may cause us to lament that the world has gone on so long without it.   All that we can do is to perpetuate our blessings for our children, and with this view I can do no less than encourage my fair friends in their new pursuit, by reviewing all the Albums which fall in my way.   I do this with the greater satisfaction, as it is partly in payment of a debt of gratitude, seeing that it was in them that I myself commenced fluttering my wings; and I feel that, like the lark, whatever height I may soar, I shall still look with an eye of affection to the nest from which I sprang.   Most fortunately does it happen, that I have not soared too far to describe it with becoming exactness, for, if the truth must be confessed, the secret of my ability was only communicated to me last week, and the admiring reader is now gazing on my first adventurous flight.

My nest—blessings on it !—it was the prettiest nest that ever was made, and the bird that fostered me was a bird of Paradise. Its eyes were as blue as the heavens, and its voice was sweet as any within them. "Dear Mr. ——," it sung, "I am sure you are a poet, and, therefore, you must write in my Album." Alas! how could I doubt? Had such a voice assured me that I was Apollo himself, I should have believed it. To drop the metaphor, which is not convenient, I took the book, which was locked, as well it might be, where there was so much to steal, and began seriously to be daunted by its costly appearance of red morocco and emblazoned Cupids. I felt that it was only meant to receive first-rate treasures, and submitted that it was hard to expose my first attempt to such a dangerous comparison. The appeal, however, was in vain. My beauty assured me that I need fear no comparison there, and gave me, as a reward for my labours, the enviable privilege of turning over as many leaves as I pleased. I will not deny that this examination gave me a good heart, for I thought it was not impossible, after all, that I might maintain my credit respectably enough; not that the articles were indifferent, but rather that the perusal of them lighted me up with unwonted fire.

It would be difficult, when staring upon the noonday, to say which ray is the most beautiful, or the most dazzling; and, if I instance a few of my brother-contributors, I must not be understood as doing it with any view of settling their claims to superiority. I merely go upon the judgment of my pretty friend, who seemed anxious to direct my attention to the lucubrations of a young gentleman who screened himself from fame under the pathetic name of Alphonso. I rather suspect he was her lover, for she described him very affectionately as a melancholy youth, who had an opinion that geniuses were not long-lived, and had made his will the moment after he had composed his first stanza. I do not wonder that the piece made him low-spirited. It ran as follows:—

Madonna, still my fount of song is hidden
    By names that are not thine; for I am one
To whom thy praises are a theme forbidden,
    Albeit so deeply, dearly learnt by none.

Madonna dear, 'tis midnight, and the blast
  Is telling of the times when thou wert here
To clasp my hand, and listen as it pass'd
  To the wild tale with which I won thine ear.

Still, still for thee this lonely hour I borrow
  To muse, if yet thy kindly thoughts remain;
And the bright eyes, that wept unreal sorrow,
  Find a fond tear for those I need not feign.

Perchance the wand'rings of a joyless heart,
  Too chilled to merit what it might not claim—
Perchance the story ne'er at loss to start
  In raven swiftness on the wounded name—*

Perchance the spirit kindled by thine own,
  Too high to plead 'gainst faults too soon allow'd,
Have swept me from thy mind, my course unknown,
  Like the sear'd leaf before the wintry cloud.

'Twere hard to blame thee, hard as to forget,
  And mem'ry still creates thy vision nigh;
Lovely and loved, and mild and melting yet,
  To list my story as in days gone by.

Come, with thy gentle hand once more in mine,
  Thy lips prepared to murmur my reward—
Come, soul of beauty, o'er my harp incline,
  And mark if grief hath left one tuneful chord.

    * Alphonso was said to have been flirting with some one
else.

Poor Alphonso ! I was given to understand that he was undoubtedly a genius, and wrote well, for it was generally suspected that he was a little beside himself. Indeed, what I afterwards saw seemed to favour this surmise, for his sentiments were occasionally inclining to be watery, just as though they had slipped through the crack in his head.

In the next page to Alphonso, my admiration was excited by a remarkably fine spashy-dashy drawing, so boldly touched that I had some difficulty in penetrating the mystery of what it meant. I was told, however, by my pretty companion, that it was an assemblage of desolate rocks and rolling clouds, with the ocean far beneath, and a rude grave in the foreground, bearing the initials of the artist, and intended as an illustration of some suicidal stanzas by the same hand. This star it appeared had likewise been shining a little too near the moon, though it was affected in a different manner. Alphonso was a gentle being, and was satisfied to fade away like a dying daisy ; but the suicide man was a determined misanthrope of the By-

N 2

ron school, and kept his friends in a turmoil
lest he should wring his own neck. He had
met with two or three disappointments in love,
and had been choused out of happiness till he
had very properly learnt to despise it. Every
thing he drew or wrote had a smack of bitterness, and was particularly fine for a bold indication of what is called freethinking ; but making designs for his grave, which were usually in
cross roads, and his numerous epitaphs, of which
I counted about twenty, were, out of sight, his
most congenial occupation. Most willingly
would I treat the reader with some of the former, but I have not yet been long enough
apprenticed to my new avocation to be much
of a hand at engraving, and the suicide's style
is very difficult to copy. I will give him one
of the epitaphs, however, and welcome.

> Ay, call me back to life again
>   With lamentations o'er my tomb——
> I cannot hear the hateful strain,
>   And, if I could, I would not come.

There is something very striking in this obstinate determination expressed in such sullen

brevity, and I could perceive a pensive irresolution in the eye of my young friend, as to which of her two heroes should be sacrificed. It no doubt requires much deliberation, and I hope and trust that she will not decide hastily. I inquired after the suicide yesterday, and found that he was still living.

After this, I was introduced to some witty conceits by a middle-aged rubicund *roué*, who cocked his hat and his eye, and set up for a wag. He practised chiefly in the Anacreontic line, and would have been excellent had he not sometimes been " a little too bad." My lady of the Album wished the odious creature would leave her book alone ; and, before I had time to become better acquainted with him, she laughed and blushed, and slapped it together, with a vow that I should not proceed unless I promised to pass him over. I regret that this circumstance prevents me from favouring the public with more than two stanzas.

> And art thou not content to view
>   My sorrows at thy feet ?
> And must I write the record too,
>   For triumph more complete ?

No, rather on this book divine
Receive my vow profound—
'Twere sweet to be a page of thine,
If cherish'd, clasp'd, and bound.

It was quite a relief to turn from this intense study to a series of flower drawings by a gentle young lady who had not been prevailed upon to exhibit without great solicitation. She was, however, one of my favourite's long string of bosom friends and confidants—the sweetest sympathizer in all her cares, and unhappily attached to Alphonso, who had doomed her, like himself, to a willow wreath. There was no doing without such a dear contributor as this, and, indeed, her performances were interesting to a degree. It was pleasingly melancholy to behold them. Her roses were as pale as if they had been in love themselves, and the butterflies which fluttered around them were one and all dying of consumptions. There was no positive colouring or touching—softness was her peculiar characteristic, and any appearance of vigour would have been rejected as absolutely indelicate. I was told that the bouquets were for the most part fashioned for the indication of some tender sentiment, or the exhibition of some beloved face which was formed by the outline of the flowers; and, after a diligent search, I found Alphonso peeping through a broken heart's-ease, and the fair artist, hard by, in a flower of love-lies-bleeding. There was an affecting simplicity in these conceits which perfectly atoned for the projectress's want of poetical talent. She had no particular knack at originality, though she was thought to select with great taste. She had copied all the performances of Hafiz and the Princess Olive from the Morning Post, and several privately circulated pieces, which were supposed to be the production of Lord Byron himself. I ventured to differ upon some of these, but my young friend satisfied me of their genuineness, by assuring me that they had been transcribed from an album somewhere near Mont Blanc.

From hence I wandered through a great many pages of excellent riddles, with which I will not treat my reader, lest he should stop to puzzle them out—numerous copies of Madonnas and children, of which the only defect was a trifling inclination to squint, it being very

difficult to make the eyes match — wondrous
landscapes by little persons of four years old,
who never learnt to draw — autographs of John
Brown and William Williams, and many other
celebrated gentlemen, whom 1 did not know,
but of whose families I had often heard talk—
fac-similies of the hand-writing of Buonaparte,
imitated from specimens from recollection—
striking likenesses of notorious characters, cut
out in coloured paper from imagination.   In
short, my progress was like a ramble through
some newly discovered country, where every
thing is rare and rivetting, and thrown together
in the graceful confusion in which nature delights.

When I had come to a close, my pretty
friend resumed her coaxing look, and besought
me to take up my pen, for she was quite sure
that I should not be eclipsed ; and, moreover,
that I should not be severely criticised.   Her
friends had the keenest eyes in the world for
talent, and could spy it in every thing they
saw ; and, if her father chose to call them all
crazy, it was a comfort to think that no one
agreed with him.   The command, therefore,

was readily obeyed, and I joined the throng of geniuses, by filling the centre of a splendid page with the following scrap of jealousy, got up for the occasion, by way of making myself interesting :

Give me again that early vow
   That ruled so long my fate—
Thy lofty look hath wandered now,
   And turns to me too late.

'Twas sweet to see the wild flower rest
   Where none the wreath might twine,
But, faded from another's breast,
   It blooms no more for mine.

BENEDETTI'S ADIEU.*

U<small>NSAID</small>, unsung, thou shalt not go,
　My native land—my own—
For, from thy vocal gale, I know
　My love of song hath grown ;

And I would crown thee with a wreath
　Of echoes, soft and sweet —
Dear land, the first to hear me breathe,
　And feel my infant feet !

Heaven reared thee with a lofty crest—
　To thee no rival rose,
In Delos, with her eagle's nest,
　Or Paros, with her snows ;

* This little poem is not original, and I know not whether
I may venture to call it a direct translation. Benedetti was
the author of a great many tragedies, which were played,
with success, at Florence, from about the year 1803 to 1820.
His life was, nevertheless, a series of misfortunes. Being, at
last, implicated in the plots of the Carbonari, he fled to Pis-
toja, and, finding himself still pressed by the police, put an
end to himself with a pistol.

And bravely o'er the boundless mead,
    By Clano's rainbow rill,
Thou seest a thousand shepherds lead
    Their myriads from the hill—

Thou seest Politian's slopes and dells
    With purple vines o'ergrown,
And Thrasymene's breast, that swells
    With ocean's distant moan—*

That lake, which Punic Hannibal
    With Latian blood imbued—
That valley, which the stormy fall
    Of Latian limbs bestrewed—

In grisly gear, 'tis said by some,
    The spectres march by night,
And, at the sound of sword and drum,
    Renew their phantom fight;

Whilst hurrying home, through pits and pools,
    From that unearthly wrack,
The ploughman shrinks to feel the tools
    That clank upon his back.

* There is said to be a mysterious sympathy between
them.

BENEDETTI'S ADIEU.

Day's waking beams for ever first
    Thy cloudless summit wins,
And there the breeze thy flowers have nurs'd
    Its vesper song begins;

Yea, softly sports, like infant sprite,
    So heedless and so fond,
Though Boreas may rudely smite
    The sheltering hills beyond.

'Tis thus thou rear'st thy rugged peak,
    And twin'st thy vintage sweet—
Thus, ne'er such bloom had summer's cheek,
    In Chios or in Crete;

Whilst, all around, the hanging rocks
    Are glittering with the gleam
Of rivulets, with little shocks,
    Down bounding to the stream.

Cortona, shall I ne'er again
    Tread where my soul so clings?
Dear land, that gave thy swan his strain—
    Ah, wherefore then his wings!

Sad, sad my gloomy planet lowers,
    Where'er my path has been;
I count a world of turbid hours,
    But never one serene!

BENEDETTI'S ADIEU.

Well I recall that night of woe,
   When, heedless of our sighs,
Our cottage reddened with the glow
   Of flames that lit the skies!

I could not choose but drop a tear
   On Ruin's wings outspread,
Which, true to yon prophetic fear,
   Still hover o'er my head.

But thou, with thy maternal hands,
   Didst calm my beating brow,
Nor was I forced to foreign lands
   To drag me hence, as now.

No wasting fever shrank my form,
   No traiterous weapon tore;
But nightly, on thy bosom warm,
   I slumbered as before.

But now, by Fortune's stern command,
   Condemned from thee to go,
I take her by the fickle hand,
   Prepared for weal or woe—

An exile, on a pathway blind,
   Beset with strange mischance;
Chill poverty and grief behind,
   And darkness in advance!

Oh ye, my own, my native hills,
    In sorrow slowly pass'd—
Ye spirits of the rocks and rills,
    That lull me to the last—

Grove, grot, and bower, and mossy spring,
    Where I no more may rest,
Receive the last adieus that wring
    Thy poet's aching breast.

Perhaps, upon some barren strand,
    I seek a bleak repose ;
Too poor for any friendly hand
    My dying eyes to close—

E'en thou, my love, wilt not be there,
    To speak my name unknown,
Or press thy gentle forehead fair
    Against th'unlettered stone.

I go, like old Laertes' son.
    In exile o'er the wave,
Through Scylla's hungry jaws to run
    To Cyclops' horrid cave ;

But oh, to him, through all his toil
    'Twas fated still to win
The hearth-stone of his native soil —
    A grave amidst his kin !

AUTHORS AND EDITORS.

Adieu, monsieur. J'avois toutes les ardeurs du monde
d'entrer dans votre alliance : j'ai fait tout ce que j'ai pu pour
obtenir un tel honneur ; mais j'ai eté malheureux, et vous ne
m'avez pas jugé digne de cette grace.

Molière.

I DARE say there are few amateurs or in-
cipient professors of literature, who do not
think that the Editor of a Magazine is the most
comfortable workman in the craft. He is not
subject to the rejections and mortifications
which sometimes fall to the lot of less potential
persons, and has the power of patronising his
friends and annoying his enemies just as much
as he pleases. All this is very true, but, to my
sorrow, I must dispute the inference. I was
once, in a dark hour of my fate, induced to
become the lord of one of these great creations
myself, and, though I was deposed immediately

after the publication of my first number, I obtained quite enough experience to turn pale at the sight of a proof-sheet ever after. I set to work with the determination of being popular, and encountered the cares and fatigues of unriddling hieroglyphic manuscripts, and patching up broken sentences, with the constancy of a literary martyr. I hunted in holes and corners for genius in obscurity, that I might display it to the noon-day, and I felt my heart warm at the gratitude with which I was about to be rewarded. I reviewed new publications, paintings, and performances of all descriptions, with the tenderness of a parent to the first pledges of his fondness; I was on both sides in politics; and I never received a communication from the veriest ass which was not attended to as punctually as a love-letter.

One would have thought that, with so many claims to universal good-will, I could not fail of obtaining it. Alas! after fidgetting and fevering myself to a skeleton, I discovered that folks of my calling are something in the predicament of house dogs, which are not only cursed for every honest bark they make, but mistrusted and vilified even when they fawn for favour. Before I was in power, I was considered a good sort of a person enough, and had as many friends as most people. I could walk the streets without thought of danger, and go about my business without fear of criticism. In one orief quarter of a year I have outfallen the fall of Phaeton. I have not only made no new friends, but have lost all my old ones. I cannot show my face without being hooted like an owl by day-light, and shall never again put pen to paper without seeing each miserable sentence drawn and quartered and hung up to public view as the remnants of the malefactor who presumed to lord it over his betters. Expostulation is out of the question. A blockhead who has undergone the scratching out of a sentence is as impatient as though it had been his eye ; a manuscript which has been returned is morally certain of becoming wadding for a pistol ; and I look upon all the obligations which I have conferred as so many thunder-bolts which are destined to crack my ex-editorial crown.

In addition to all these grievous circumstances, the numerous assurances which I have received of the fallibility of my judgment have altogether destroyed the confidence which I used formerly to repose in it. I feel shy of hazarding an opinion upon the merest trifle, for fear it should be disputed. My taste, vision, and hearing, seem totally different from those of other people ; and had I not materials to prove what I have here advanced, I doubt very much whether I should have ventured to say a word upon the subject. Fortunately, when I commenced my editorial functions, I bought a huge bandbox to hold contributions. The favours of my friends soon crammed it to splitting ; but, when store-houses of this kind come to be threshed out and winnowed, it is astonishing what a cloud of chaff is produced for every particle of solid grain. My whole treasury was expended in my one campaign, and I set about filling my box (which has been the very box of Pandora in every thing save the article of Hope) with the first fruits of it. It is now, if possible, fuller than it was before, and, if the reader likes the samples I am about to give him, I will feast him as long as he has an appetite. The first *morceau* I have laid my hand upon is from a gentleman to whom I wrote——" The Editor of the —— Magazine presents his compliments to Mr. ——, and begs to offer his best thanks for the perusal of his Essay on Pathos, which he regrets exceedingly his great supply of that article obliges him to return."

The reply to this polite billet is as follows :——

" Sir,

" I am extremely glad to have my Pathos again, as it was only sent for the support of a Magazine which has no chance of succeeding by its wit. At the same time, I must inform you that it was a matter of some condescension for a person so well known as myself (in private circles) to submit my works to the judgment of one who is only likely to be conspicuous from his incapacity to appreciate them. My friends, upon whose taste I can fully rely, are of opinion that my Essay on Pathos has great power, for it was read before them a month ago, and they have been dull ever since. This, however, is not said that you may send for it back, and I think it right to

inform you that I shall listen to no future soli-
citations to write for the —— Magazine ; and
remain, Sir,   Your's," &c., &c.

One would have thought that the indignation
of this lover of dullness, with whom I had the
misfortune to feel so little sympathy, would at
any rate have been counterbalanced by the
kind words of those whose effusions I had
printed in preference.   But no such thing.
The same post brought the following from a
young beginner, a block fresh from the timber-
yard, who had intreated that I would do him
the favour of lopping and chopping him just
as I thought best; and I vow that, in my
fatherly anxiety for his reputation, I spent
more time upon his lucubrations than I did
upon my own.

" Sir,

" 'The articles which I sent to your
Magazine having been so changed and deprived
of all point, and, consequently, so abused by
every one who has read them, I am, of course,
perfectly free to disown the authorship.   I

consider them to be *your* production, and, in justice to my reputation, shall take the liberty of giving you the credit of them.

"I am, Sir," &c., &c.

Again, in another hour, would arrive the cursed twopenny-post-man, with his sharp tap at the door, which made me start as though it had been a dead shot, and I was overwhelmed with a flight of notes, that croaked like a congregation of ravens.

"Sir," said one evil genius, "you have done me a serious injury by reserving my article for the next month, for the interest of the subject will have entirely gone by."

"Sir," said another, "by not giving me an answer respecting the article which I sent you the day before yesterday, (a moderate-sized volume) you have obliged me to decline a very liberal offer for it; therefore, I consider you bound to take it, whether you like it or not."

"Gentlemen," said I, in a pathetic circular, "permit me to remind you that the —— Magazine is a book and not a library, and, by this oversight in arrangement, totally incapable of

devouring all your wits at a meal.   Allow me
to submit, at the same time, that some of the
bits are terribly tough, and that it is no fault
of mine if the public are not ostriches."

Such malecontents as these, I believe, cannot
fail of being thought a little unreasonable, but,
if so, what will be said of the next epistle,
which was written by a son of Apollo, whom I
had lauded out of pure friendship to his calling?

" Sir,

" I have just seen in your Magazine a
review of my poem, which you clearly do not
understand, and of which you have materially
injured the sale by misleading the public opinion.   You call it sublime, when, in fact, it is
pathetic.   People are tired of the sublime, and
the comparison with Milton is ruination to me.
I will defy you or any one else to find a single
passage which might be mistaken for Milton's.
You call it harmonious, when it is meant
to be abrupt and impassioned throughout.
You call the conclusion to the story moral and
edifying, when nothing can be more the reverse.   In short, you have played the deuce with

all its greatest beauties, and the consequence is that nobody will read it.

"My friend Mr. ———, the artist, is with me, and begs that you will not mention his picture again, having put him to great inconvenience in contradicting all that you have said. It is not like Claude, or Nature, or any thing else, but is entirely original. The colouring is upon a new principle, and is not transparent, but opake throughout. The figures are *not* well drawn, but are touched off with a graceful negligence, and, instead of an evening scene, it is intended to be sun-rise.

"I remain," &c. ———.

I could now, if I were not afraid of making the reader as tired as I was myself, give scores of letters from authors who were anxious to propitiate the favourable judgment so despised by the foregoing. I could lend him a library of all sorts of literature, which was sent to me with the choice passages marked for quotation. Nay, I could guide his judgment by reviews of which the sagacity is not to be doubted, for I am morally certain that they proceeded from the same pens with the works which they eulogized. Then I could give him letters of recommendation from brother editors, who were anxious to get rid of their refuse contributors; requests from various friends that I would provide employment for supernumerary young gentlemen, who, having a great love for idleness, were thought by their families to be especially cut out for poetry and the *belles lettres*. Moreover, as a convincing proof of my high consideration for the said benevolent reader, I will indulge his kind heart by turning over to him the young gentlemen themselves. They will probably be men of great performance, for there is not one amongst them who condescends to be a man of promise.

As if all this had not been enough to transfer me from Grub Street to Bedlam, I had to sustain the good advice of mine own familiar friends, who were one and all so anxious for my success that they sent me more communications than all my tormentors put together. They reminded me that the —— Magazine was the hothouse in which my budding talents had been forced into blossom. Again, that I was a mere genius in the shell when Fortune had deposited me in that publication——that my worthy publisher was the bird that had hatched me and watched the growth of my wings, and that I was bound to imitate the young stork, by bearing him upon my shoulders into wealth and prosperity. This being the case, they took the liberty of offering a few suggestions; which, for the most part, were in direct opposition to each other. Then, one would have the record of births, marriages, and deaths; another the price of stocks; a third, fashions; a fourth, politics; and a fifth, advertisements. All this might have been extremely reasonable, but there was one slight inconvenience in it which was totally overlooked. When the hedgehog got into the hole, the snake was obliged to turn out; and this must have been the case with the Belles Lettres.

The foregoing is a mere taste of my treasures. I have complaints, and revilings, and expostulations, and challenges, and all sorts of entertaining things, on every subject and in every style imaginable; but what I have already given is quite enough to maintain my opinion of editorial comfort.

To my sorrow, however, my literary miseries and mortifications were, as I have already stated, not the only ones for which I had to call upon the consolation and sympathy of the benevolent. Some of these collateral sufferings were the hardest of all, and, as nothing affords such a relief to the afflicted as a kind ear into which he may pour his history, I must take leave to hold the reader by the button for yet a few last words.

When I first took office, the celebrity of the Magazine was a fair guarantee for the talent and taste of the new editor, and my heart was elated by invitations to every house in town where those qualities were most estimated and patronized. I thought myself (and I believe my mistake was very common to most other folks in my station) a very superior character, and considered that, as I was to lead the public judgment, it was incumbent upon me to show my capabilities. Besides, I knew I was asked out in order that I might entertain the company, and do credit to those who introduced me. A great deal was expected of me, and I never liked to cause disappointment if I could help it. I used to take pains to be a brilliant talker. The blue stockings got to think me an oracle, and I never made my appearance without being surrounded by a coterie of delighted listeners, as though I had been a crier on a market-day, or a juggler at a fair. My opinions were adopted, my *bon-mots* repeated, and I had the reputation of half the good things which had been said by other people. I was "the glass of fashion," and used to see myself at second hand in troops of young aspirants who thought to steal into the temple of Fame in masquerade. Alas! the triumph was of short duration; my wits broke down under my cares. I had started from my zenith and was on the wane from the first. I went to my displays with a sore heart and a nervous dread of finding society as fastidious respecting my opinions as I had found my legion of authors. I began to think that the attention bestowed upon me was to ascertain how much nonsense I could talk, and that all my listeners were laughing in their sleeves. When a man doubts himself he is sure to be doubted by every one else. All those who had never ventured to think anything right or wrong till they had looked to me for the cue, were heard to decide for themselves, to differ with me, to argue, and to make their case good. I was considered a vapid composition of small beer, with a little froth when I was first poured out, and nothing but deleterious drugs behind. Parties were given to which I was not invited, and I felt that general opinion denounced me as a stupid dog, and that all who had been so lavish of their praises were obliged to retrieve their credit by retracting every word.

This, it will be said, was a gradual decline, and that I had, at all events, the comfort of preparing for its termination, as folks usually do for a natural death; but I was doomed to die more deaths than one, and some of them were shockingly sudden. I had been intreated, in my outset, to suffer my name to be put up as a candidate for various literary clubs; had been pampered with delightful descriptions of the wit and harmony of the gifted brotherhood; and had boasted to all my acquaintance of my intention to belong to them. There was, however, a fatal regulation that all names should be placarded a certain time before election, that people might have an opportunity of seeing whether there was any "just cause or impediment" against them. I really forgot upon how many of these Newgate calendars I stood for trial, but I remember perfectly well that, when the several ordeals arrived, I had more black balls than white in every one of them. I was so crest-fallen that, for a long time afterwards, I hardly dared show my visage in a common chop-house, for fear of being kicked out. All the world thought I had done something wrong, and my current name in society was the Knave of Clubs.

Not only did I hate to be seen, but I was doomed to be informed that I was not *fit* to be seen, for a celebrated painter, who had requested that I would add to his reputation by giving him a few sittings for the next exhibition, found it necessary to regret, in the politest manner possible, that his press of business obliged him to put me off *sine die*. This was another bitter blow, for we had made arrangements for a beautiful *mezzotinto* engraving, of which, in my fulness of pride, I had promised a copy to every young lady I knew, and I had luxuriated in the contemplation of all the new discoveries of wit, sentiment, and sagacity, which would be made in my editorial expression.   How my heart panted to see myself staring out of a gilt frame in a shop window, with a score or two of pickpockets standing round to attract a crowd! How comfortably had I made up my mind to join the throng and hear the opinions passed upon me! Alas! in a short month, I would as soon have seen myself in the pillory!

All this was beyond human endurance; and it was a matter of choice whether I should retire from the world of letters or hang myself. My ambition was entirely gone, and I set myself seriously to consider the evanescence and the vanity of fame, which he who obtains it living is pretty sure to survive, and to which he who receives the amends of its posthumous justice is insensible. I called to mind that the greatest genius in the world had described it as a bubble, and that the wit of Falstaff himself could discover no one who possessed it but " he that died o' Wednesday." My resolution was made up.

> Sae I gat paper in a blink,
> An' down gaed stumpie in the ink,

and, in another minute, away went the following appeal to the tender heart of my publisher. Had I waited another post, I have no doubt he would have taken measures to spare me the trouble.

"Dear Sir,

"It is with deep regret that I feel myself under the necessity of resigning my high and honourable post, which requires qualifications to which I have no pretensions ; for I have neither the quills of the porcupine nor the hide of the rhinoceros. Should the gentleman whom you may be pleased to appoint as my successor be desirous of any hints descriptive of the community over which he is destined to preside, I shall have great pleasure in gratifying him ; it will also be a heart-felt satisfaction to turn over to him a large pile of contributions, which I trust will suit his purpose, for I really have not nerve to send them back to their owners. If any one should inquire for me at your house, pray be good enough to have him bound over to keep the peace. The state of my health renders it absolutely necessary that I should go to some retired watering-place, where I may enjoy, without molestation, the benefits of sea-bathing and ass's milk.

Believe me, dear sir,

—— ——.

THE MOORISH BARQUE.

Licosa, 'tis a lovely thought
   That roams thy rocky steep,
Where palms and wild pomegranates wrought
   Sweet shades for summer sleep;
And blossom'd aloes rear'd the head
   Like guardians of the grove,
To shield it from intrusive tread
   Of any step but love.

I dream upon the dawn serene,
   When on thy seaward crag reclined,
I saw by cleft and rude ravine
   Thy bird-nets waving in the wind,
And weary wings far o'er the sea
   From burning suns and barren sands,
Faint flutter to a worse decree
   In cruel captor's hands.

I would I could recall as well
   The latent urchin's lay—

The long wild lay, that rose and fell
   As came the fitful prey—
'Twas but the tale so often told
Of maiden fair and lover bold,
Rich in all gifts excepting gold,
And hopeless as the hearts of old;
   But yet so wild the strain,
That lingering memory still would hold
   The fragments that remain.

Bold peasant youth, fair vintage maid,
Their love was laid in Fortune's shade,
That thing so pure might never fade,
   Nor lose the simple pride,
Whenever task romantic fell,
By vine-clad rock, or orange dell,
   Of toiling side by side.

'Twas eve; and one had gained his prayer
Of toil to take the double share
   Beneath the sultry ray;
And one had chased the lonely hour
With love-songs in her mossy bower,
   Fair beetling o'er the bay.

'Twas gentle eve, the task was done,
   And now, like wild-dove on the wing,
He sought the smile his pains had won,
   Beside the star-lit spring.

And swifter still his course he took,
  For ne'er those pains had been
So distant from the lovely look,
  Such weary hours unseen —
And as he went he thought how oft,
When waves were calm, and zephyrs soft,
The stranger sail would linger there
For water from the fountain fair,
  And fancy wilder grew
On all that savage hands might dare,
  And all that love might rue ;
When hovering on the outward breeze,
  Beneath the mountain dark,
Behold the falcon of the seas—
  Behold the Moorish barque !

A moment, and he reached the grot
  Where she had lain, but lay not now ;
And broken wreath, and true love knot,
And footmarks by the fountain plot,
Full plainly spoke the maiden's lot —
  The prize of yonder prow !

His thrill was like the lightning shock,
  His thought the bolt in flight :
A bound, and he hath cleared the rock,
  Like sea-bird swooping from the sight ;
And o'er the tide behold him take
His pathway in the pirate's wake.

Far, far away from bower and beach
　　His desperate course he bore,
'Till gasping swimmer ne'er might reach
　　Its rock of safety more.——
On, on he went, and onward, too,
　　The barque was lessening from his view,
Till pitying zephyrs seemed to grow
All breathless at the sight of woe,
　　And the fleeting sail
　　Sunk down to sleep,
　　And a voice of wail
　　Came o'er the deep——
A voice, with Heaven's especial charm,
Once more to nerve his failing arm.

His hand is on the pirate's stern.
　　His piteous plaint hath brought
The Pagan band, unused to burn
With human love, to look and learn
　　What deeds that power hath wrought.

" I am a peasant," thus he spake,
　　" These hands the token bear ;
I have no hope but her ye take,
No wealth beyond the heart ye break,
　　No ransom but my prayer.
Then think upon my fate forlorn,
And take, oh take, these limbs outworn,
Nor listen to my grief with scorn,
　　Because ye do not share.

" Ye cannot tell, oh ye who reign
   O'er captives from the cruel mart,
How dear the office to sustain
Toil, sorrow, poverty, or pain,
   With love's confiding heart —
How dear the wedded hopes that thrall
The soul to which those hopes are all,
How mutual chains can never gall,
   Like diadems apart."

   They listened to the suppliant's prayer,
      And raised him to the deck,
And stood in silence round the pair,
To marvel that a maid so fair
      Clung round a Christian neck.
And then the breeze, which late was spent,
Sprang up again, and on they went,
Still sailing to the low lament
      Of joy's untimely wreck.

  " Oh whither, whither, dost thou rove
      Beneath the midnight sky ?
  And wherefore hast thou stolen the love
      Of peasant poor as I ?

  " Take back, take back my promised bride,
      Weak hands for toil hath she,
  And I will work the double tide,
      And bless thee on my knee !"

THE MOORISH BARQUE.

"The wind doth waft us fresh and free,
    The planets brightly lead
  To Tunis or to Tripoli,
    Where'er we best may speed.

"And we have stolen thy bride away
    To bear no peasant's paine,
  But grace the harem of the Bey,
    Whom thou shalt serve in chains."

'Twas morn : a hundred warriors press'd,
  With vest of gold and visage grim,
Before the judgment seat, and guessed
The price of beauty's beating breast,
  And love's devoted limb :
And the dark chief, with omen dread,
Gazed long upon the maid, half dead,
Until her hero's tale was said,
  And then he gazed on him.

And as he gazed he seemed to tell
  How heaven ne'er oped the flower of fear,
But kindly, in its poison bell,
It left some honey drop to dwell,
  The guardian of the sphere.
Yea, how the winds and waves can die
In whispers, like a love-born sigh,
And the wild lightning skim the sky,
  Upon a calm career.

And mild he spake—" I will not wound
  One plume your soaring hopes possess'd,
Nor cast our lawless links around
Two hearts the King of Kings hath bound
  Into a shrine so blest.
There rather shall the Moor lay down
A tribute worth his ruby crown,
That ye may rule to love's renown
  The land ye love the best."

Oh whither, whither, once again,
  Bold pirate, dost thou hold
Thy course upon the bounding main,
  With freight of gems and gold ?

And who are these that trust the wave
  Beneath thy dreaded sail ?
This pair, so beautiful and brave,
  That chide the lagging gale ?

Vain question for an answer guess'd !
  For pains and perils past,
Behold once more Licosa's crest,
  Where love is crowned at last.

There late a moss-clad column bore
This simple page of peasant lore,
  And aye, at vintage eve,
Young plighted pairs dreamt o'er and o'er
  What love might still achieve.

END OF VOL. I.

EDITED BY THEODORE HOOK, Esq.,

AND ILLUSTRATED WITH A PORTRAIT OF THE LADY
CHARLOTTE BURY.

THE FIRST NUMBER FOR 1837, OF

COLBURN'S

NEW MONTHLY MAGAZINE,

EDITED BY THEODORE HOOK, ESQ.,

WHO COMMENCES THE NUMBER FOR JANUARY WITH

THE GURNEY PAPERS.

THE NEW PUBLICATION ANNOUNCED UNDER THE TITLE OF

THE HUMORIST

is, at the suggestion of Mr. Hook, incorporated with the New
Monthly, and forms a prominent feature of Wit and Comi-
cality in that Magazine, which is accordingly increased in
quantity, and contains various other improvements.

N.B. With the exception of an article promised to another
Journal, Mr. Hook will in future confine his periodical writing
to the New Monthly.

PRINCIPAL CONTENTS OF THE JANUARY NUMBER.

The Gurney Papers. No. I. By Theodore Hook, Esq.

THE HUMORIST:—

The Manager's Room at Little Pedlington. By John Poole, Esq.

Achates Digby. By Alfred Crowquill.

The Grand Kentucky Balloon. By One of the Authors of "The Rejected Addresses."

The Disasters of Carfington Blundell, Esq. By Leigh Hunt, Esq.

Songs of the Blacks. By J. B. Buckstone, Esq. 1. The New Jim Crow. 2. A Nigger's Reasons.

Moralities for Families. By Douglas Jerrold, Esq.

Club Law—Christmas, &c.

Retrospections, and Anticipations for 1837.

The late George Colman, his Wit and Genius.

The Mother's Heart. By the Hon. Mrs. Norton.

A Tale of the Voyage of Hendrick Hudson. By N. P. Willis, Esq.

Subjects for Pictures. By L. E. L.

Recreations on Natural History, No. 1.

Memoir of the Lady Charlotte Bury (with a Portrait).

Notes on Literature, the Arts, &c.

State of Agriculture and Commerce.

HENRY COLBURN, Publisher, 13, Great Marlborough Street.

TO BE HAD OF ALL BOOKSELLERS IN THE KINGDOM.

F. SHOBERL, JUN., LEICESTER STREET, LEICESTER SQUARE.

CPSIA information can be obtained
at www.ICGtesting.com
Printed in the USA
BVHW090931270819

556819BV00014B/3113/P